Physical Characteristics of the Bolognese

(from the Fédération Cynologique Internationale breed standard)

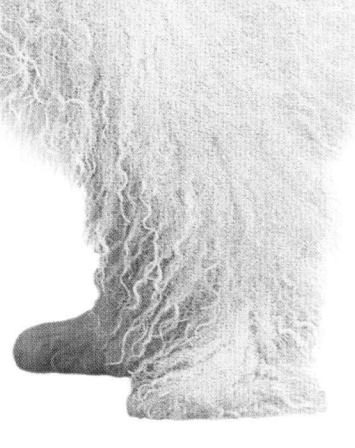

Body: The dog being of a square construction, the length of the body, measured from the point of the shoulder to the point of the buttock bone is equal to that of the height at the withers.

Hindquarters: Considered on the whole and viewed from the back, they must follow from the point of the buttock bone to the ground a perfectly vertical line.

Tail: Set in the line of the croup, carried curved over the back.

Color: Pure white.

Coat: Long all over the body, from head to tail. It is shorter on the muzzle.

Height: At the withers—Males: 27 to 30 cm, Females: 25 to 28 cm.

Weight: From 2.5 to 4 kg.

Bolognese

◇

By Wolfgang Knorr

Contents

9   **History of the** Bolognese

Italy's contribution to the bichon breeds, the small white Bolognese has a noble history as the pampered pet of royalty. Travel the globe to meet the Bolognese's bichon relatives, meet the breed's illustrious owners and see how the breed was re-established following World War II in its homeland and across the Atlantic.

28   **Characteristics of the** Bolognese

A companion beyond compare, the Bolognese's only purpose has been and still is to be the best possible friend to humans. Learn about this fascinating white bundle of charm by discussing the breed's physical and personality traits, the best type of owner for a Bolognese, things to do with your Bolognese and more. Are you and the Bolognese a perfect match?

36   **Breed Standard for the** Bolognese

Learn the requirements of a well-bred Bolognese by studying the description of the breed set forth in the Fédération Cynologique Internationale standard. Both show dogs and pets must possess key characteristics as outlined in the breed standard.

44   **Your Puppy** Bolognese

Find out about how to locate a well-bred Bolognese puppy. Discover which questions to ask the breeder and what to expect when visiting the litter. Prepare for your puppy-accessory shopping spree. Also discussed are home safety, the first trip to the vet, socialization and solving basic puppy problems.

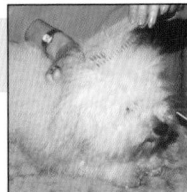

68   **Proper Care of Your** Bolognese

Cover the specifics of taking care of your Bolognese every day: feeding for the puppy, adult and senior dog; grooming, including coat care, ears, eyes, nails and bathing; and exercise needs for your dog. Also discussed are the essentials of dog ID, safe travel with your pet and boarding.

Training Your Bolognese

92

Begin with the basics of training the puppy and adult dog. Learn the principles of house-training the Bolognese, including the use of crates and basic scent instincts. Get started by introducing the pup to his collar and leash and progress to the basic commands. Find out about obedience classes and training for other activities.

Healthcare of Your Bolognese

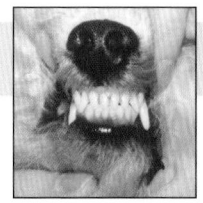

113

By Lowell Ackerman DVM, DACVD
Become your dog's healthcare advocate and a well-educated canine keeper. Select a skilled and able veterinarian. Discuss pet insurance, vaccinations and infectious diseases, the neuter/spay decision and a sensible, effective plan for parasite control, including fleas, ticks and worms.

Showing Your Bolognese

140

Step into the center ring and find out about the world of showing pure-bred dogs. Here's how to get started in dog shows, how they are organized and what's required for your dog to become a champion. Take a leap into the realms of obedience and agility trials and more.

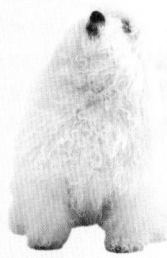

Index 156

KENNEL CLUB BOOKS® BOLOGNESE
ISBN: 1-59378-350-7

Copyright © 2007 • Kennel Club Books® • A Division of Bowtie, Inc.
40 Broad Street, Freehold, NJ 07728 USA
Cover Design Patented: US 6,435,559 B2 • Printed in South Korea

Library of Congress Cataloging-in-Publication Data
Knorr, Wolfgang.
  Bolognese / by Wolfgang Knorr.
    p. cm.
  ISBN 1-59378-350-7
  1. Bolognese dog. I. Title.
SF429.B634K56 2006
636.72--dc22   2006011621

10 9 8 7 6 5 4 3 2 1

Photography by: Carol Ann Johnson
with additional photographs by:

Paulette Braun, Bernd Brinkmann, Carolina Biological Supply, Isabelle Français, Zoila Portuondo Guerra, Bill Jonas, Dr. Dennis Kunkel, Tam C. Nguyen, Phototake, Ian and Mary Poulter, Jean Claude Revy, S. Symes and Alice van Kempen.

Illustrations by Patricia Peters.

The publisher wishes to thank all of the owners whose dogs are illustrated in this book, including Christel Buchmann, Merle DeMoss, Carol Doanne, Marsha England, Barbara Garayalde, Claudia and Wolfgang Knorr, Lascaris and Liz Stannard.

The Bolognese is a rare breed, but those lucky enough to know these dogs love them! Looking at this happy face, it is easy to see the breed's appeal.

HISTORY OF THE

BOLOGNESE

Although an ancient pure-bred of noble origins, the Bolognese today is regarded as a rare breed in most countries of the world. Much speculation exists about the possible origin of this bichon breed, though ultimately its true origins remain obscure and are likely never to be revealed fully. With an irresistible face characterized by "three black buttons," the Bolognese represents the Italian version of the popular bichon-type dogs, although it most certainly did not originate there. The Bolognese belongs to the ancient aristocracy of dog breeds, but where did the history of the Bolognese actually begin?

Small white dogs were already known of when the Phoenicians and ancient Egyptians were traveling around the Mediterranean. Along the trade routes of the seafarers, the "small whites" traveled from coast to coast as precious cargo of the peripatetic Phoenicians. From some point in time during the 13th century, these seafarers also brought white dogs to Italy, where their small size enchanted the region's royalty and aristocracy.

A GENUINE ITALIAN TREASURE

Throughout the centuries of its history, the Bolognese has always been a very special breed. It was the declared favorite of royalty and aristocracy. Its fascinating and affectionate character leaves no doubt among fanciers and breeders that this small dog with its white curly coat represents a genuine treasure.

Select breeding of these dogs began soon thereafter, with the name *Bolognese* being derived from the ancient Italian city of Bologna, where these small white canines appealed to many dog lovers.

Traders were fully aware of the little white dogs' value, and specimens were sometimes even paid for with their weight in gold. It was considered a partic- ular symbol of wealth to be seen with such a little snow-white beauty. The dogs were the declared favorites of well-born Italian women and became mandatory "fashion accessories" for the ladies of the aristocracy. The absolute favorites in drawing rooms, the Bolognese were spoiled, powdered and perfumed, and their coats, often adorned in cords, were trimmed according to the latest fashion. In general, the dogs were given so much attention that the French verb

bichonner, which means to "to pamper," gave rise to the breed's initial name, *Bichon Bolognais*. The breed became known as the Bolognese some time later.

The Gonzagas, a noble family that ruled parts of Italy between 1328 and 1708, were known to have bred Bolognese in their palatial estates. Even the Medicis valued these little dogs, and Cosimo dé Medici (1389–1464), the affluent, influential Florentine citizen who became the city's most important patron of the Italian Renaissance, has been recorded to have at one time sent no less than eight Bolognese pups to Belgium, where his emissary Nuntius gifted the dogs to a select few rich and mighty nobles. You might say that the tiny but mighty Bolognese thus started to conquer the whole of Europe from Italy.

Many historical personalities ensured that they were seen with this little dog that embodied luxury, examples being the Madame la Marquise de Pompadour (1721–1764), Catharine the Great of Russia (1729–1796) and Maria Therese, Empress of Austria (1717–1780), who were all proud owners of these little beauties. The dogs' popularity continued during the times of Kings Louis XIV and XV of France and endured well into the 19th century, and old

Empress Elizabeth of Manchukuo, wife of the former "Boy Emperor" of China, strolling in her garden with her Italian toy dog. Photo circa 1930s.

A lovely pair of modern-day Bolognese. As adults, the male (left) is a bit larger than the female (right).

From the early 1930s, this photo of a Bolognese was captioned "An almost perfect specimen."

masters, such as Gozzoli and Dürer, immortalized them in many paintings. Commoners had no chance whatsoever to own one of these small dogs.

As history teaches us, all good things must come to an end (or at least an indefinite hiatus). Quite suddenly, or so it seems, this famed and revered breed of dog fell from favor, along with the downfall of Europe's aristocracy.

By the end of World War II, the Bolognese had become almost extinct, with only a handful of breeders in the world, including in Italy where the breed had once risen to fame. If the records of the Italian breeding register are to be relied upon, the first modern Bolognese were registered by the kennel of Sna. Maristella Ogno in the late 1950s.

BICHONS IN RUSSIA
During the 18th and 19th centuries, Russia had become an important part of international trade relations under the rule of the czars. In this time period some dogs had also reached that country who would become historically significant, though not to the Bolognese. As a result of the Bolshevik Revolution in October of 1917, which disposed of the czars, many countries discontinued their friendly trade relationships with Russia. Thus

The Russian Bolonka Zwetna breed is seen in many colors and shades. It is related to the bichon breeds as well as other popular toy breeds.

isolated, no additional dogs came into the country, forcing breeders in the new Union of Soviet Socialist Republics (USSR) to develop a separate breed that became known as the *Bolonka Franzuska*, while the development of the Bolognese was continued in Italy. In other words, the Bolognese was being bred in western Europe and the Bolonka Franzuska in eastern Europe.

Parallel to the western European Bolognese, the Russian Bolonka Franzuska (meaning

THE SOVIET BICHON SPINOFFS

The Bolonka Franzuska was considered a separate dog breed in the USSR. It is still unclear whether it is related more closely to the Bichon Frise of France or to the Bolognese of Italy. The Bolonka Franzuska is responsible for a spinoff known as the Bolonka Zwetna, a new bichon breed not recognized by the Fédération Cynologique Internationale. The Bolonka Zwetna was developed by crossbreeding the Bolonka Franzuska with the Pekingese and Shih Tzu in the early 1950s.

"lapdog from France") was bred in the former German Democratic Republic (East Germany) without receiving international recognition through the Fédération Cynologique Internationale (FCI), the international kennel club to which most Continental countries belong. These Russian-bred bichons showed only little resemblance to their presumed ancestors from France or Italy, with the only common feature being that both breeds had white coats of curly hair. The Bolonka Franzuska breed had been developed in the USSR and found its way, mainly via diplomatic channels, into the then-aligned East Germany.

The breed had a large number of fans who continued to breed these dogs in Germany for many decades. The last dog show open to entrants and visitors from the West was held in Leipzig in 1964, after which the Iron Curtain to the Federal Republic of Germany (West Germany) also fell, hindering all dog-sport activities involving the two Germanys. This meant that breeders in East Germany could not access fresh blood from the West to invigorate their bloodlines but were limited to their own and Russian stock. Their breeding potential was therefore severely limited. As a result, the individual bloodlines

The Russian representatives of the bichon family: on the left is a Bolonka Franzuska, which shares its white coat with the Bolognese. A pair of Bolonka Zwetna are shown at center and right.

A pair of beautiful Bichons Frise. This breed has a white coat like its Italian cousin, but a major difference is the Bichon Frise's grooming style, in which the coat is meticulously sculpted into shape.

of the Bolonka Franzuska continually became more closely related, and inbreeding eventually commenced. As emphasis was more on breeding numbers rather than on breeding quality, the Bolonka Franzuska gradually but constantly grew smaller, with more and more faults in comparison to their ancestral lines. In the early 1980s, the committee of the East German dog breeders' association attempted to have the Bolonka Franzuska registered by the FCI using the standard for the Bolognese. However, the charac-

teristics of the two breeds were too different, and the Bolonka Franzuska was not granted the same level of recognition that the Bolognese breed was already enjoying.

The fall of the Berlin Wall, which had separated East and West Germany, on November 9, 1989 also meant a drastic turnaround for the Bolonka Franzuska as a breed. Not even a year later, on September 23, 1990, the members of the former East German dog breeders' association were assimilated into the West German society of small-breed dog breeders, which in turn formed part of the VDH (Verbandes für das Deutsche Hundewesen, [the German Kennel Club]), which became an established member of the FCI. In the process, the pedigree records relative to the Bolonka Franzuska were indiscriminately rewritten to conform to the recognized Bolognese breed.

THE FAMILY OF BICHONS

Besides the Bolognese, the Maltese, Bichon Frise, Coton de Tuléar, Havanese and Löwchen form the family of bichon breeds. The Maltese, which probably represents the oldest breed of bichon, is considered the type representative of all bichons. It is unfortunate, though, that its exact history, like that of the Bolognese, cannot be completely reconstructed today. The oldest record of a Maltese in the Mediterranean region was unearthed during archeological work in Egypt. Greek vases dating from 500 BC also depicted small white fluffy dogs. During its entire history of development, the Maltese was considered a jewel among dog breeds.

During the course of centuries, if not millennia, the appearance of the Maltese with regard to its coat changed a number of times. It was certainly all but exempt from the continu-ously changing fashion trends and therefore at times may have looked quite different from what we today know as the Maltese, "a pure-bred dream in white."

The Bichon Frise, originally known as *Bichon Ténérife*, also originated in the Mediterranean region. Spanish seafarers had brought the breed, acting as trade goods, to the Canary Islands, and when it was later returned to Europe, it promptly turned into a favorite lapdog of the Spanish and Italian aristocracies. The Bichon

A modern Maltese, showing off the breed's long, straight white coat.

Mrs. Stallibrass, one of the Maltese's staunchest supporters, with one of her "Maltese Terriers," as the breed was known at the time. Circa 1902.

Frise became known for its high trainability and intelligence. It was therefore often trained to perform a variety of tricks and was highly popular with the *clochards* (the classic French hobos) as a means to beg for money. The Bichon Frise was registered in France only in 1934, and the breed is inseparably linked to the outstanding breeding efforts of Mme. Carmen Desfarges and her kennel De La Buthière.

The Coton de Tuléar, on the other hand, is a temperamental, joyous breed of bichon from Madagascar. The history of this enchanting small dog is as romantic and speculative as any

THE RAINBOW OF BOLOGNA
Today the Bolognese is found only in white without markings of any kind. Historically, however, the Bolognese was not always just white but also existed in various colors including black, brown and tan. Today among the bichon breeds, the Havanese and Löwchen are seen in a variety of colors, but the Bolognese, Bichon Frise, Maltese and Coton de Tuléar are seen in solid (or mostly) white.

other breed in the family portrait. One legend tells that small bichon-like dogs were kept for rat control onboard pirate

The Coton de Tuléar is a related breed from Madagascar known for a soft, cotton-like coat.

ships operating in the Indian Ocean early in the 16th century. Shipwrecked, some of these dogs managed to swim to the shores of the island of Madagascar, where they later mixed with native dogs. Other sources claim to be certain that European settlers brought dwarf *épagneuls*, Maltese or Bolognese to Madagascar, where they interbred with the indigenous island dogs. In any case, the Bichon Ténérife, transported by trade ship, reached the island of Réunion, where, likely through genetic adaptation, it developed its characteristic soft, cotton-like coat. Known originally as the Coton de Réunion, the small dog later became almost extinct on that island. A few surviving specimens were eventually relocated by traders to the port city of Tuléar on the south-western coast of Madagascar. The Coton de Tuléar was recognized as a breed only in 1970 and is therefore considered a young breed.

Like some of the other breeds of bichon, the Havanese, or *Bichon Havanese*, has several theories of its origin. One of many hypotheses claims that the predecessor of the Havanese was the *Blanquitto de la Habana*, which was a Spanish bichon-like dog. Another theory holds that the Havanese developed in the

The modern Havanese on the Malecon of Havana, Cuba, photographed by the protector of the breed in its homeland, Zoila Portuondo Guerra.

The Havanese in America is groomed a bit differently from its Cuban counterparts.

Mediterranean region, and transatlantic ships were responsible for its early introduction into Cuba.

The Havanese was most commonly seen with a tobacco-colored ("havana") coat, and this led to the presumption that it actually originated in the capital of Cuba, Havana. While this is not the case, the breed did become very popular in Havana. Due to the Cuban revolution, many Havanese dogs left the country with their owners. The handful that came to the US survived and established new bloodlines here. Today the breed is flourishing in the US and is recognized by the American Kennel Club.

Rooted in France, the Löwchen, nicknamed the Little Lion Dog or Petit Chien Lion, is a small breed of bichon, closely related to the Maltese. While the

EARLY BREED TYPES

Before the individual breeds of bichon were bred selectively, hardly any distinct traits separated them, and breed names abounded. In the 16th century, all types of small white dogs were referred to as either dwarf *épagneuls*, from which today's Papillon was developed, or as Maltese.

THE BOLOGNESE IN AMERICA
BY AMY FERNANDEZ

Dorothy Goodale is credited with introducing the Bolognese to America. She had bred dogs for 45 years, beginning with Beagles, Poodles and Soft Coated Wheaten Terriers, before she became interested in rare breeds. With her husband Bert, she imported the first Havanese into the US from Cuban refugees and established their world-famous Berdot Havanese kennels. She first became aware of the Bolognese during the 1970s, while researching all five of the Bichon breeds. "I kept coming across references to the Bolognese during my research, at the library or in correspondence with foreign breeders. The more I read, the more curious I became," says Dorothy. She was especially intrigued by the fact that this was the only Bichon variety that had never been imported to the US.

The Löwchen is closely related to the Bolognese. The very appropriate breed name comes from the German word meaning "little lion."

breed is not well known around the world, there is a considerable growing interest in the US and UK. The Löwchen resembles the Maltese and Havanese very closely and even more so the Coton de Tuléar. Its coat is traditionally clipped short on the rump so that the dog assumes a lion-like appearance. The breed fell out of fashion early in the 20th century, when this sculpted leonine look did not quite conform to the prevailing taste of the day. As with the other bichon breeds, the Löwchen's origins can be traced back to early medieval times. Two stone sculptures in the cathedral of Amiens, France clearly represent Little Lion Dogs, whose coats are trimmed to resemble those of lions, very much in the same fashion as Löwchens are trimmed today.

A LUMP IN HISTORY
Dr. Hillebrecht published an article in the December 1898 issue of the magazine *Zwinger und Feld* that provided sound evidence that the Bichon Frise originated in the Canary Islands. It describes how a small woolly Poodle with the name of "Lump" was brought from the island of Tenerife to the city of Antwerp in Belgium.

Dorothy began writing to various European kennel clubs to request the addresses of Bolognese breeders in Europe. Through this correspondence, she learned of the Vansteenkiste kennels in Belgium. Madame Gerde Vansteenkiste-Delen was among the first breeders attempting to re-establish the Bolognese. She founded one of the world's most influential Bolognese breeding programs in the 1970s and helped popularize the breed by extensively campaigning her dogs throughout Europe. Although she has now retired, her bloodline continues at the Van Het Vogelpark kennels, also located in Belgium.

Like many breeds, the Bolognese gene pool had been decimated during World War II. The breed had nearly died out and, 30 years later, breeders were still working to re-establish viable Bolognese populations in their own countries. The Goodales were able to locate three European breeders—one in Denmark, one in Germany and one in Belgium—but all of them were understandably reluctant to export dogs. It took a couple of years before Dorothy was able to convince one of them to part with any of their valuable Bolognese stock.

She was finally able to import the first Bolognese into the US in 1986. Her original foundation stock came from six different

countries, beginning with two pairs of dogs from the Danish Ja-Birs kennels of Jan and Birte Warming. The first two dogs, an unrelated male and female, were soon followed by two more female puppies. Additional imports came from Italy, Denmark, Belgium, Germany and Portugal, including dogs from Italian breeders Carla Peronda and Alberto Veronesi.

She fell in love with the breed immediately. "This is the smartest breed I have ever worked with.

Part of the Bolognese's beauty is his white coat, which is left in a natural state—no trimming allowed!

They do great in obedience but tend to become bored with repetitive exercises. They absolutely love agility. The Havanese are smart and very good dogs, but Bolognese are different. People who claim that dogs cannot reason have never lived with a Bolognese. I suspect that they are telepathic. They are great problem solvers."

Dorothy began breeding her Danish imports when they were about 18 months old but ran into a problem common to many rare-breed fanciers. "We could not get people interested in the breed. We knew the Bolognese were wonderful dogs, but no one knew what they were."

Dorothy remained the only US Bolognese breeder for several years, and her bloodline is the oldest established Bolognese breeding program in the US. In 1987, the Goodales founded the Bolognese Club of America (BCA) to promote and protect the breed in the US. The club began with approximately ten founding members, a combination of the Goodales' puppy-buyers and interested Havanese breeders. The club provided a forum to bring Bolognese owners together and offer assistance to fanciers in the US. Dorothy and Bert also established the first US Bolognese registry, which Dorothy still maintains today.

Although the BCA remains the largest US Bolognese registry, the club has never pushed for American Kennel Club (AKC) recognition. According to breeder Melissa Scheetz (Aspen Villa Bolognese), "We love placing our puppies as pets first." Melissa has worked closely with Dorothy for the past three and a half years, taking over raising her Bolognese and Havanese. She began her own breeding programs for both breeds two years ago and also assists Dorothy with the club's registry and newsletter.

Most of the original BCA members remain affiliated with the club today. BCA breeders in

Although currently a rare breed, the Bolognese will surely attract many followers in the years to come.

the US and Canada continue to import new bloodlines from Hungary, the Czech Republic and Italy. BCA-accredited breeders are required to have their dogs' eyes tested and certified with the Canine Eye Registration Foundation (CERF) and have their dogs' patellas (knees) tested, both annually. No major genetic problems have been noted in the breed to date, although breeders vigilantly monitor their dogs for eye health and knee stability. All breeding stock is tested annually and only healthy dogs are used for breeding.

The BCA has adopted the FCI (Fédération Cynologique Internationale) standard for the Bolognese. Melissa points out, "Because the Bolognese is still in its infancy, you see many different-looking Bolognese." She notes that the only major change in breed type that has occurred in the US in the past two decades is a reduction in size. "A good average size for Bolognese is 8 pounds." The FCI standard permits a weight range of 5 to 9 pounds. The BCA also publishes a bimonthly newsletter, *The Band Wag-on,* and funds a nationwide rescue league. To learn more about the BCA, visit them online at http://members.aol.com/Bolognese America/bca.htm.

BCA member Carrie Belair (K'Bella Bolognese), from Cumberland, Ontario, Canada,

founded the Bolognese Club of Canada in 2005. Other organizations that recognize the breed in the US today include the United Kennel Club (UKC), the American Rare Breed Association (ARBA), the AKC's Foundation Stock Service (FSS) registry and the Bichon Bolognese Association of America (BBA).

The BBA was founded in 2000 by Johan and Diane Hesseltvan Dinter of Spice of Life Bolognese in Wisconsin and Sharon Todman of Fatima's Bolgnese in Bakersfield, California. Members of the BBA are actively seeking AKC recognition for the breed. They support the development of an internationally recognized Bolognese and adhere to the Italian and FCI standards. The BBA maintains a registry and breeder referral service and publishes a club newsletter. For more information,

Sired by Julien Von Weiben Kindertraum and out of Amanda Von Albany, this is Fabiola Von Albany of Sopra Villa kennels.

Ch. Amanda Di Chiesanova, of Sopra Villa kennels, was sired by Elisea and is out of Trottola.

you can visit the club's website at www.bologneseclubus.com.

Johan and Diane Hesseltvan Dinter acquired their first Bolognese in 1992 from Dorothy Goodale and began breeding and exhibiting in 1995. "Shortly after we started breeding," notes Diane, "we became aware of the range of variability in the breed, especially in terms of size. This was not confined to American bloodlines. Italian breeders were experiencing the same problems. And the northern European Bolognese tended to be larger than the Italian dogs." Diane and her husband decided to import new stock in hopes of creating a more consistent type within their line.

In May 1996, they traveled to Europe with the intent of finding and importing quality Bolognese from unrelated bloodlines. With the help of various European contacts, they were able to locate breeders and purchased two puppies, one from Italy and one from the Czech Republic. Both of these dogs had a major impact on their breeding program. Their Czech import, Brize Cesky Dukat, was already a Czech champion and went on to earn his ARBA championship in the US. Since then, they have continued to

import Bolognese from Italy, Belgium and the Netherlands. One of their most notable imports was a Dutch champion, Roxanne, who unfortunately died prematurely but managed to pass her exceptional structure and movement on to her progeny.

Today there are approximately 500 to 600 Bolognese in the US, and the breed remains free of health problems. "We are not yet a big club," says Diane. "I am satisfied with our rate of growth. Membership has doubled in the past three years." She is concerned about the potential problems that may accompany popularity as the breed gets closer to AKC recognition. "Our foremost concern is that our dogs have good homes."

Other US breeders making major contributions to the breed today include Marsha England of Renaissance Bolognese in Colorado; Sharon Todman of Fatima's Bolognese in California; Barbara Garayalde of Sopra Villa Bolognese in Idaho; and Carol Doane of Prelude to Joy Bolognese in Washington.

The breed has gained a following in Britain. This Bolognese is volunteering his time and charm at a booth for the British parent club.

Spice of Life Estella Expectation, commonly known as Estee, is the sister of ARBA Master Ch. Spice of Life Artful Dodger and now resides at Prelude to Joy kennels.

PERSONALITY

The Bolognese has been bred over centuries for one purpose only—to be a companion to people. This remains the breed's purpose in life today. Its very charming character is in fact a major identifying feature of the breed. Paired with an enchanting appearance, the Bolognese's winsome ways enable him to captivate many of his fans. Notwithstanding this, it would be not quite fair to consider him a mere lapdog. The Bolognese is a dog of true quality, a big-dog personality in a small package. He will be very affectionate toward his owner, and he is not reserved in showing the world that he has a "big heart," quite in contrast to his small physique.

The Bolognese will even turn out to be a good watchdog and show surprising bravery if necessary, without being a yapper. Despite his diminutive size, he has a pleasantly deep voice, so his occasional barking should not bother your neighbors. He never works himself up into

A Bolognese puppy can't get close enough to his loving family. This is Prelude to Joy Gilligan with Kailynn Doanne.

The overall appearance of the Bolognese should be that of a small dog, balanced in height and weight, and just about square in proportion.

the persistent, ear-piercing yelping that some other small dogs are known for.

Families with children will truly enjoy the playful ways of the Bolognese. Once he has been taught to remain at home alone, he is content to stay at home for three or four hours at a time. His need for activity is limited, but he enjoys walks with his owner just as much as relaxation on the couch. He is a delightful little dog with an extraordinary ability to adapt, happy to stay by his owner through thick and thin.

The Bolognese is highly intelligent and teachable, finding pleasure in obedience exercises and training. His even temperament makes him an ideal dog for an apartment or small home, and he is equally suited for young and elderly owners. He is neither headstrong like a Dachshund nor obstinate like a Shih Tzu. He is simply amicable and abundantly affectionate and loyal toward his human companions.

All of these traits render the Bolognese easy to train with positive reinforcement, as he is rarely in need of scolding. As with any other dog breed, a harmonic, happy coexistence of dog and owner results from education, understanding and unconditional love.

The all-white coat is a trademark of the breed, although keeping it white can indeed be a challenge.

A PORTRAIT OF THE BOLOGNESE

SIZE

According to the FCI breed standard, the adult Bolognese weighs 6 to 9 pounds. The author is not in complete agreement with the weights as indicated in the standard, believing that they are impractical given the height of the dogs. A female Bolognese is permitted to be between 10–11 inches high, a male can be 10.5–12 inches at the withers. The dog's weight should be complementary to height, especially to achieve an overall balanced appearance. The author's experience demonstrates that a male dog in proper condition, standing 12 inches at his withers (highest point of the shoulder), weighs about 13.5 pounds, considerably more than the upper weight limit in the standard. Such a typical

Irresistible as pups and adults, Bolognese are a lot of joy in a little package.

LOOKS AND CHARM

The Bolognese is marked by large round dark eyes, which contrast with a coat of pure white long hair with a soft and fluffy texture. With his squarish build, the Bolognese is a small, well-proportioned dog with a long, soft, fluffy coat. His face is dominated by his black-bordered dark eyes and his pitch-black nose. These "three black buttons" in the middle of a cloud of white will enthrall those who meet the breed time and time again.

male dog proves why the author does not endorse the FCI standard's size requirements. In terms of size, the Bolognese resembles the Bichon Frise very closely, with the latter also not exceeding 12 inches in height as per the FCI standard. A standard formerly used in the US set more realistic guidelines for the Bolognese with the following: "Males from 10 to 12 inches at the shoulder; females from 9 to 12 inches at the shoulder. The weight averages from 8 to 14 pounds.

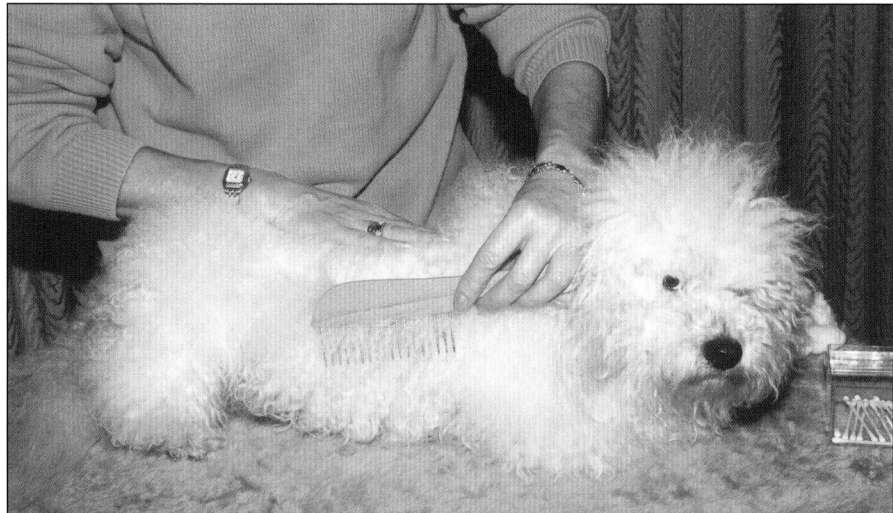

The Bolognese does not require trimming or fancy grooming techniques but does need time devoted to coat maintenance, something to which owners must be ready to commit to before owning the breed.

Mid-weight and mid-height are considered the most desirable."

CHARACTER

The FCI breed standard's description of the breed's character makes the point that the Bolognese is a calm and docile dog with strong attachment to his humans. Of course, no description can accurately describe every member of a breed, as all dogs are individuals, just as their owners are. The author has found the breed to be rather serene and calm, though, from personal experience, the author can tell you without reservation that a Bolognese is well capable of displaying a lively and funny demeanor. Some breed members possess a comportment very similar to that of the Poodle, and they may sometimes act like little clowns, taking much pleasure in amusing the family.

"Teachable" is an accurate term when discussing the Bolognese. This is a small dog that enjoys activity and training lessons. He is in fact always eager to learn something new. He is calm and perceptive, which are excellent traits that are much

TO CLIP OR NOT TO CLIP

If the coat of your Bolognese appears to be overly frayed, the tips of the hair may be clipped every now and then. For show purposes, a Bolognese must never appear as though he has been clipped, especially in the sculpted manner of a breed like the Bichon Frise. As a puppy, the coat may be trimmed between the ages of four to six months, which improves the strength and stability of the hair.

appreciated by an owner when training his dog. Despite the Bolognese's academic prowess, he is still first and foremost a companion dog. His loyalty to and affection for his owner are legendary. His major task is to love his human partner and in return receive love from him. The Bolognese always strives to please his owner.

Although the Bolognese isn't known to be an avid swimmer, he will enjoy activity time with his owner.

Coat

The Bolognese has a coat of long, dense hair that may appear slightly bristly, because it stands off from the body. The entire body of the dog has the appearance of being covered with curly fleece. Soft and fluffy with a lot of undercoat, the hair is very long on the head and limbs, while it is less profuse on the face and muzzle. The hair on the tail falls like a curtain over one side of the hindquarters. A Bolognese is always pure white, although puppies may exhibit a slight tinge of champagne on the ears and body. These insignificant "stains" usually disappear as the dog grows older. Any color other than white is stated in the FCI standard as a fault that disqualifies a Bolognese from showing.

The breed's wonderful curly white coat of hair does not require intense care in order to maintain its superior qualities, whether on a show dog or a pet. In contrast to his closest relative, the Bichon Frise, the Bolognese's coat must never be trimmed. He is everything but a styled dandy, and his coat is basically left as it grows naturally, even if this might lend him the appearance of a rather unkempt dog. Regardless, it is advisable to shorten the coat of a Bolognese a few times when he is still young, as this improves the curliness and stability of the hair. Regular combing, brushing and bathing make up the most important routine coat-care procedures. You will hardly find a more gentle character in a dog, and if you are prepared to spend about 30 minutes of your time at least 3 or 4 times a week grooming your dog, there should not be any obstacles in the way of your long and happy friendship.

ACTIVITIES FOR YOUR BOLOGNESE

Dog sports aren't just for big dogs anymore! Seeing small dogs competing in obedience and agility trials is nothing out of the ordinary these days. Sport-oriented owners may therefore consider a Bolognese as a suitable, adaptable, active companion. Many training schools offer training courses for Canine Good Citizen® certification, and some have classes specifically for small dogs. These same schools may also offer training classes to prepare for obedience and agility competition. Agility exercises challenge owners and their four-legged companions to master a series of obstacles. The exercises on a course include such fun obstacles as the collapsible tunnel, seesaw, weave poles, dog walk and tire jumps. All of these require skill and can be a lot of fun for the well-trained Bolognese and his owner, too. Trained by qualified instructors, the owner learns how to guide his dog through the course and the dog learns how to handle the obstacles properly.

With the Bolognese being a small companion dog, all activities should be understood as play and fun. Unlike working or herding breeds, the Bolognese lives for fun and pleasure (not for moving sheep or guarding estates). Because agility trials are no doubt challenging for the Bolognese, the owner should never demand too much of his dog or force him to continue with something he does

If taught how to properly interact with one another, children and the Bolognese can be great friends.

not enjoy. Dogs are never trained for agility before one year of age. Of course, a basic education (including obedience commands and general good manners) is a prequalification to beginning agility training.

THE BOLOGNESE WITH CHILDREN
For most children, there is nothing as exciting as having a new pet. Dogs are among the most popular companion animals and, when well chosen, can comple- ment perfectly the life of a family with children. Having a dog must, however, be the decision of the parents. It is also their responsi- bility to educate their kids with regard to raising, feeding and caring for the dog. Never should it be made the responsibility of the children alone to look after the family's four-legged companion; ultimately it remains the responsi- bility of the parents to ensure the well-being of the dog.

The Bolognese likes children, though it is not the best choice for a family with children, especially children who are too young to grasp the concept of how to treat an animal properly. Given the small size and relative daintiness of the breed, owners must instruct children about how to handle the dog carefully. Puppies are much more fragile and are entirely unsuitable for young children. Nevertheless, if

you are convinced that the Bolognese is the breed for you (and your family and children), then careful supervision and responsible education can make all the difference in the world. Include the children in caring for the dog. Children can be taught how to brush the Bolognese's coat, though the actual grooming, a fairly demanding chore, must rest with the parents. Take the children to the pet-supply store to shop for the dog's food and other necessities; have the child assist in giving the puppy a bath; teach the child how to walk the puppy on the leash; and make the child responsible for checking the dog's water bowl. All of these simple chores will teach a child respon- sibility while at the same time building the child-dog bond that can be so rewarding to the lives of both of them.

Bolognese are small and adaptable dogs that fit in well with many types of people and places.

BOLOGNESE

The Fédération Cynologique Internationale (FCI) stipulates that a breed's standard should be written by the fanciers from the breed's country of origin. In certain cases, however, the country that introduced and promoted the breed can be granted the "country of origin" rights. The standard should describe in detail what the ideal representative of the breed should look like. The purpose of the standard is to convey to breeders, fanciers and dog-show judges all of the important features of the breed, the essential traits that "define" the breed.

The first standard for the Bolognese was written in Italy in 1929. Since then, various changes and additions have been effected, the most important of which are credited to Sre. Sularo (1971). Notably, the standard changed the maximum size of the Bolognese to about 30 cm (about 12 inches) at the shoulders. It is thus a small, compact, squarish dog, which should not at all be considered as a "dwarf" breed. It is worth noting that the Bolognese was little known in

Western Europe at the time. The latest version of the FCI breed standard for the Bolognese came into effect on November 27, 1989. It was translated by Peggy Davis and is presented here.

FCI STANDARD FOR THE BOLOGNESE

TRANSLATION
Mrs. Peggy Davis.

ORIGIN
Italy.

DATE OF PUBLICATION OF THE ORIGINAL VALID STANDARD
27.11.1989.

UTILIZATION
Companion dog.

CLASSIFICATION
Group 9 (Companion and Toy Dogs). Section 1 (Bichons and related breeds). Without working trial.

BRIEF HISTORICAL SUMMARY
Its origins are confused with those of the Maltese, because its distant ancestors are the same little dogs mentioned in Latin by

Aristotle (384–322 BC) under the denomination of *canes melitenses*. Already known in the Roman era, the Bolognese appears most especially among the very appreciated gifts which were made during a whole era by the powerful of that world. Cosimo de Medici (1389–1464) brought no less than eight to Brussels as gifts to as many Belgian noblemen. Philip II, King of Spain from 1556 to 1598, after having received two as a gift from the Duke d'Este, thanks the donor in writing, saying that "these two little dogs are the most royal gifts one can make to an emperor." Bolognese are represented in paintings of Titian, of Pierre Breughel called le Vieux and of Goya.

GENERAL APPEARANCE
Small size, stocky and compact, covered with a pure white coat, long and fluffy.

IMPORTANT PROPORTIONS
Square built, the length of the

A head study showing correct type, structure and proportion with a mature natural coat.

body being equal to the height at the withers.

BEHAVIOR/TEMPERAMENT

Very serious, generally not very active. Enterprising, docile, very much attached to his master and his entourage.

HEAD

Of medium length reaching one-third of the height at the withers. Its width, measured at the level of the zygomatic arches, is the same as its length.

Cranial Region: *Skull*: Of slightly ovoid (egg-shaped) shape in the sagittal direction and rather flat in its upper part, has rather convex sides; the protuberances of the frontal bones are well developed. The longitudinal axes of the skull and muzzle are parallel; the frontal furrow is only slightly accentuated and the occipital protuberance only slightly marked. The length of the skull is slightly more than that of the muzzle. *Stop:* Rather accentuated.

Facial Region: *Nose:* On the same line as the topline of the muzzle; seen in profile, its front side is on the vertical. Is large and must be black. *Muzzle:* Its length is equal to 2/5 of the length of the head; the topline of the muzzle is straight and the sides of the muzzle are parallel, so that the forepart of the muzzle is almost square. The lower orbital region is well chiseled. *Lips:* Upper lips being hardly developed in depth, they do not cover the bottom lips, and the lower profile of the muzzle is determined by the lower jaw. *Jaws/Teeth:* Jaws normally developed, with top and bottom arches perfectly adapted. Teeth white, evenly aligned, with strong and complete dentition. Articulation of incisors as scissors bite; pincer bite tolerated. *Eyes:* Set on an almost frontal plane; well opened, of superior to normal in size. Eyelid opening is round; the eyeball must not be prominent; the white of the eye is not visible. The rims of the eyelids must be black, and the iris of a

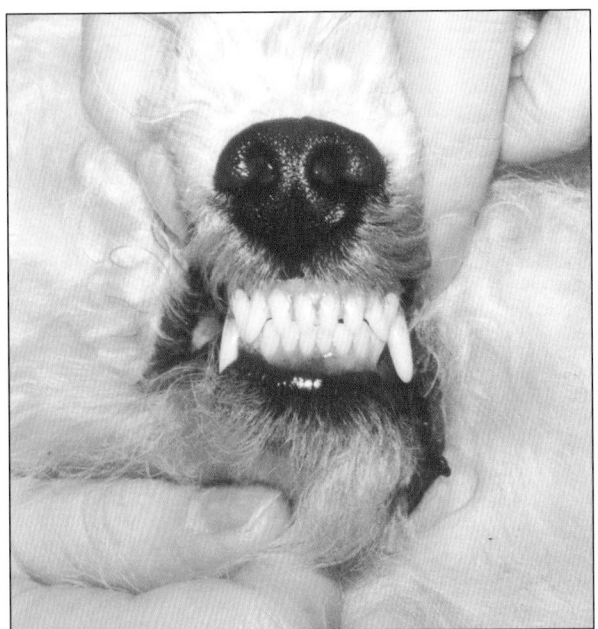

The adult bite of a mature Bolognese.

Adult Bolognese in profile showing the correct type, structure and proportion with a correct natural coat.

dark ochre color. *Ears:* High set, they are long and hanging, but rather rigid at their base, so that the upper part of the external ear is detached from the skull, giving thus the impression of the head being larger than it really is.

NECK
Without dewlap; its length is equal to the length of the head.

BODY
The dog being of a square construction, the length of the body, measured from the point of the shoulder to the point of the buttock bone, is equal to that of the height at the withers. *Withers:* Only slightly prominent from the topline. *Topline:* The straight profile of the back, and that of the loin, slightly convex, merge harmoniously in the line of the croup. *Croup:* Very slightly sloping; is very wide. *Brisket:* Point of the sternum (manubrium) only slightly prominent. *Chest:* Ample, let down to level of elbows, with well sprung ribs, the height reaching almost half of the height

at the withers. *Underline:* Following the profile of the sternum, then rises slightly towards the belly.

TAIL

Set in the line of the croup, carried curved over the back.

LIMBS

Forequarters: Considered on the whole, they are perfectly straight and parallel in relation to the median plane of the body. *Shoulders:* The length of the shoulder blades is equal to one-quarter of the height of the withers; in relation to the horizontal, they are slanting and are near the vertical in relation to the median plane of the body. They are well free in their movements. *Upper arm:* Well joined to the body, of an almost equal length to that of the shoulder, but less slanting. *Elbows:* They are on a parallel plane to the median plane of the body. *Forearm:* Its length is equal to that of the upper arm; follows a perfect vertical direction. *Pastern joint and Pastern:* Seen from the front, they continue the vertical line of the forearm. Seen in profile, the pastern is a little bit slanting. *Forefeet:* Oval shaped, with well cushioned dark pads and very hard black nails.

Hindquarters: Considered on the whole and viewed from the back, they must follow from the point of the buttock bone to the ground a perfectly vertical line—they are parallel to each other. *Upper thighs:* Their length is equal to one-third of the height of the withers. They are slanting from top to bottom and back to front and perfectly parallel to the median plane of the body. *Lower thigh:* Is longer than the upper thigh. *Hock joint:* The tibia-tarsal angle is not very closed. *Hocks:* The distance from the point of the hock to the ground is slightly less than a third of the height at the withers. *Hind feet:* Same characteristics as the front feet, but less oval.

BETTER THAN THE AVERAGE DOG

Even though you may never show your dog, you should still read the breed standard. The breed standard tells you more than just physical specifications such as how tall your dog should be; it also describes how he should act, how he should move and what unique qualities make him the breed that he is. You are not investing money in a pure-bred dog so that you can own a dog that "sort of looks like" the breed you're purchasing. You want a typical, handsome representative of the breed, one that all of your friends and family and people you meet out in public will recognize as the breed you've so carefully selected and researched. If the parents of your prospective puppy bear little or no resemblance to the dog described in the breed standard, you should keep searching!

COMPARISON OF BOLOGNESE IN PROFILE

The standard calls for a squarely built dog, but the typical dogs are slightly longer than tall. Without the mop of curly white hair, the dog shown here is structurally sound.

Many pleasing specimens are proportioned like this structurally sound dog, which is longer than tall. This can be accentuated by a heavy coat of white curls.

This dog is square, but many of the specimens so balanced are not particularly sound. The dog is high in the rear, is weak and narrow both in front and rear, lacks angulation at both ends, is ewe-necked and has a long narrow muzzle.

The coat can hide a multitude of faults. This dog is overall too heavy and coarse, short-necked and bullish in front, with a soft topline, low tail set and a narrow stilted rear.

GAIT/MOVEMENT
Free, energetic, with a noble and distinguished head carriage.

SKIN
Well taut and welded to the body all over, the visible mucous membranes and the third eyelids strictly pigmented black.

COAT
Hair: Long all over the body, from head to tail, from the top line to the feet. It is shorter on the muzzle. Rather fluffy, thus not lying flat, but in flocks; never forms fringes.

Color: Pure white, without any patches nor any shades of white.

SIZE AND WEIGHT
Height at the withers: Males: 27 to 30 cm. Females: 25 to 28 cm. *Weight:* from 2.5 to 4 kg.

FAULTS
Any departure from the foregoing points should be considered a fault and the seriousness with which

The Bolognese is a double-coated breed with white curly locks covering the head and body. This dog hails from the breed's Italian homeland.

A show Bolognese from the Netherlands, where the FCI breed standard is used.

the fault should be regarded should be in exact proportion to its degree.
- Strabismus (squinting).

SERIOUS FAULTS
- Accentuated convergence or divergence of the upper longitudinal axes.
- Convex muzzle (Roman nose).
- Prognathism, if it alters the outer look of the muzzle.
- Size under 25 cm and more than 33 cm in males and under 22 cm or more than 32 cm in females.

ELIMINATING FAULTS
- Aggressive or overly shy.
- Depigmentation of the nose.

- Nose of any other color than black.
- Undershot mouth.
- Bilateral depigmentation of the eyelids.
- Wall-eyed.
- Tailless.
- Shortened tail whether natural or artificial.
- Any other color than white.
- Patches and flecks.

Any dog clearly showing physical or behavioral abnormalities shall be disqualified.

N.B. Male animals should have two apparently normal testicles fully descended into the scrotum.

BOLOGNESE

SELECTING YOUR PUPPY

Once you have met a Bolognese, you will be convinced that there is no more delightful, trainable and affectionate creature on the planet. However, you cannot make a decision about owning one simply by reading a book on the breed (no matter how lovely the illustrations). You must make an effort to meet as many Bolognese and their devoted owners as possible. Although the breed is not recognized by the American Kennel Club currently, it is exhibited at shows held by the United Kennel Club (UKC) and rare-breed organizations (like the American Rare Breeds Association [ARBA] and International All-Breed Canine Association of America [IABCA]). In England, the breed has Interim status, meaning that it is recognized by The Kennel Club (as part of the Toy Group) but cannot yet earn a championship. On the Continent and beyond, the Bolognese is shown at FCI shows in Group 9 for Companion and Toy Dogs (Section 1, Bichons and related breeds).

The Bolognese Club of America (http://members.aol.com/BologneseAmerica/bca.htm) can direct interested parties in North America toward responsible breeders and shows around the country. In England, potential owners should contact the British Bolognese Club (www.bolognese.org); club officers and contact information are listed on the club's website.

Selecting a rare breed like the Bolognese has its plusses and minuses. There is certainly a *molto bene* plus in choosing a fabulous Italian companion dog, especially when you are sure to have the first Bolognese on your

With those sweet faces looking at you, how do you make a level-headed choice?

block. While locating a litter of Bolognese will require more effort than finding a litter of Maltese or Poodles, you can be reasonably assured that, once you have found a breeder, you will not have to be concerned about poor ethics or overbreeding. Popular breeds commonly suffer from profiteering breeders who are trying to make fast money by selling puppies. You can be sure that nobody is trying to make instant *lire* by selling Bolognese in your neighborhood.

Visiting a rare-breed show is the best way to meet Bolognese

This Bolognese pup would have made a great Toto, don't you think?

FINDING A QUALIFIED BREEDER

Before you begin your puppy search, ask for references from your veterinarian and perhaps other breeders to refer you to someone they believe is reputable. Responsible breeders usually raise only one or two breeds of dog. Avoid any breeder who has several different breeds or has several litters at the same time. Dedicated breeders are usually involved with a breed or other dog club. Many participate in some sport or activity related to their breed. Just as you want to be assured of the breeder's qualifications, the breeder wants to be assured that you will make a worthy owner. Expect the breeder to interview you, asking questions about your goals for the pup, your experience with dogs and what kind of home you will provide.

people and their beautiful dogs. Networking makes all the difference in buying a rare breed. Breeders like to meet potential owners, especially if the owners show real interest in the breed and really want to proceed responsibly in selecting and caring for a puppy. Discuss any health problems that may be present in the breed. The bichon breeds and many other small dogs are affected by eye problems and patellar (kneecap) luxation, so you should ask about these. Ask the breeder about grooming and coat care, as well as his involvement in dog shows, trials and the breed club. Breeders love to "talk dog," and they are usually responsive when potential owners show sincere interest in their breed and the sport. If you are interested in obtaining a future show puppy, make sure to indicate

A SHOW PUPPY

If you plan to show your puppy, you must first deal with a reputable breeder who shows his dogs and has had some success in the conformation ring. The puppy's pedigree should include one or more champions in the first and second generation. You should be familiar with the breed and breed standard so you can know what qualities to look for in your puppy. The breeder's observations and recommendations also are invaluable aids in selecting your future champion. If you consider an older puppy, be sure that the puppy has been properly socialized with people and not isolated in a kennel without substantial daily human contact.

this to the breeder. Not every Bolognese is worthy of being exhibited, but in a breed as small in number as the Bolognese, breeders are always encouraged to know that owners will put in the effort to show their dogs. Dog shows are the main forum for the public to see a breeder's stock. When a puppy wins a ribbon, it's a feather in the owner's cap as well as the breeder's.

DOG OR BITCH?

Before you decide on which puppy to purchase, you have to make a decision about whether you would prefer a male or a female dog. Males are said to be less affectionate than females. Females, on the other hand, may be more problematic due to their being in season ("heat") twice a year. While pet bitches should be spayed (and pet males neutered), dogs of either sex who will be shown must be kept sexually intact. Both are generalizations but still contain a grain of truth— emphasis here lies on "a grain." It is a fact that, no matter which breed, male dogs are somewhat larger, stronger and more dominant than females. This is a natural phenomenon and absolutely normal. It has, however, given rise to the prejudice that a male dog would be more self-absorbed and as a consequence less affectionate. In the case of the Bolognese, as with most small dog breeds in particular, male dogs are just as compliant and trainable as females. The fact that there is no difference between the sexes in this regard is probably due to the Bolognese's particularly pronounced devotion to their human companions.

For the dog to thrive, the Bolognese must not be left alone for inappropriate lengths of time, since this would be sure to cause him (or her!) to become naughty. Males and females are no different in this regard, and misbehavior in a Bolognese can usually be traced back to mistakes committed by the owner.

According to my personal experience, some male dogs are even easier to handle than females. They are more easily trained for dog shows and display more interest in presenting themselves in a show ring. Male dogs most often attach themselves to the woman of the house.

Changes in the comportment of male dogs may in particular be noted in spring and fall, as these are the times when most bitches come into season. Males may then become more restless, may not feed as eagerly as usual and may want to spend more time outside in the hopes of meeting a "hot" female. (Incidentally, a female dog in season can be protected from being harassed by males with special tablets and sprays.)

Most bitches come into season for the first time between 6 and 12 months of age. From then on, a heat cycle occurs about every six months, with some substantial variation being possible in individual females. A season lasts for about 21 days, during which period the female should be kept on leash at all times when outside to prevent an unwanted mating.

Messes in the home are unlikely, since a healthy female will keep herself clean. If you want to be extra sure, buy some "hygiene panties" for your female to wear during the heat cycle, available from pet shops. These should be of a type that still allows the female to preen herself, as otherwise her instinct for cleanliness would be disrupted.

A season reaches its peak between days 10 and 15, and it is at this time that you have to be particularly careful to keep the female away from a male. It is also the period when the female actively tries to find a male dog. If all measures seem to fail during this interesting period of time, you will have to resort to a few tricks. For example, if you take your female for a walk, you should carry her for part of the way when you leave your home and do the same on the way back as you are approaching your home. This helps to spare the male dogs, at least in the immediate vicinity of your home, from the heartbreak

Breeder Liz Stannard with a seven-week-old puppy. To a good breeder, every puppy is a treasure.

caused by distinct scent marks made by your bitch.

LITTER SIZE

Generally, Bolognese do not have large litters, so one must be patient if they wish to acquire one of these rare little pups.

Another factor that affects puppy availability is litter size. In the author's experience, litters vary from one to six puppies. There are small bitches that produce up to six pups in a litter, and there are big, strong ones that have only

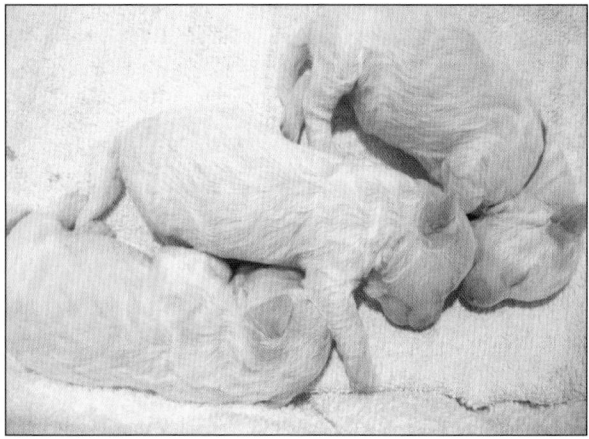

one or two. The author believes that the time in which the bitch is mated is the key factor in determining litter size; the number of eggs ready for fertilization has a major influence on the size of a litter. In order to fill the demand for puppies by enthusiastic newcomers to the breed, breeders have aimed for larger litters. Attempts by breeders to increase the number of pups by choosing females whose ancestors had large litters failed. While selecting a compatible male and female is important, there are many other factors that play crucial roles. It is the author's philosophy that the number of pups in a litter should not be a priority. What is most important is that a breeder chooses a male and a female from good bloodlines in order to obtain healthy pups that come as close to the breed standard as possible.

With regard to the Bolognese as a breed as a whole, a healthy female in good condition will have litters of three or four pups on average. This moderate litter size must be considered a reasonable success for both the female dog and the breeder. Large litters, often preferred by larger-scale breeders, mean a lot of stress for the dam, and it is not uncommon that the breeder has to assist with raising the pups as early as during the suckling phase. Main emphasis should therefore lie on a

COST OF OWNERSHIP

The purchase price of your puppy is merely the first expense in the typical dog budget. Quality dog food, veterinary care (sickness and health maintenance), dog supplies and grooming costs will add up to big bucks every year. Can you adequately afford to support a canine addition to the family?

healthy litter, first and foremost, even if this means a small litter, which the mother dog can raise herself without problems and full of confidence.

A COMMITTED NEW OWNER

By now you should understand what makes the Bolognese a most unique and special dog, one that may fit nicely into your family and lifestyle. If you have researched breeders, you should be able to recognize a knowledge-able and responsible Bolognese breeder who cares not only about his pups but also about what kind of owner you will be. If you have completed the next step in this exciting journey, you have found a litter of quality Bolognese pups.

A visit with the puppies and their breeder should be an education in itself. Breed research, breeder selection and puppy visita-tion are very important aspects of finding the puppy of your dreams. Beyond that, these things also lay

the foundation for a successful future with your pup. Puppy personalities within each litter vary, from the shy and easygoing puppy to the one who is dominant and assertive, with most pups falling somewhere in between. By spending time with the puppies, you will be able to recognize certain behaviors and what these behaviors indicate about each pup's temperament. Which type of pup will complement your family dynamics is best determined by observing the puppies in action within their "pack." Your breeder's expertise and recommendations are also valuable. Although you may fall in love with a bold and brassy male, the breeder may suggest that another pup would be best for you. The breeder's experi-ence in rearing Bolognese pups and matching their temperaments with appropriate humans offers the best assurance that your pup will meet your needs and expectations.

It will be a while before these three-day-old puppies are ready to join their human family.

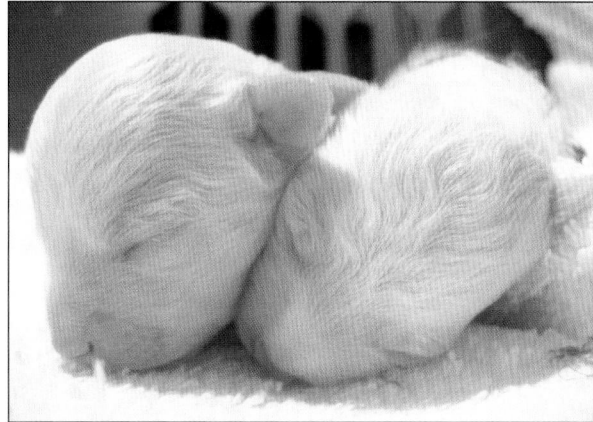

A Bolognese is an exuberant bundle of puppy love and puppy energy—are you ready?

The type of puppy that you select is just as important as your decision that the Bolognese is the breed for you.

The decision to live with a Bolognese is a serious commitment and not one to be taken lightly. This puppy is a living sentient being that will be dependent on you for basic survival for his entire life. Beyond the basics of survival—food, water, shelter and protection—he needs much, much more. The new pup needs love, nurturing and a proper canine education to mold him into a responsible, well-behaved canine citizen. Your Bolognese's health and good manners will need consistent monitoring and regular "tune-ups." So your job as a responsible dog owner will be ongoing throughout every stage of his life. If you are not prepared to accept these responsibilities and commit to them for the entire lifetime of your dog, then you are not prepared to own a dog of any breed.

Although the responsibilities of owning a dog may at times tax your patience, the joy of living with your Bolognese far outweighs the workload, and a well-mannered adult dog is worth your time and effort. Before your very eyes, your new charge will grow up to be your most loyal friend, devoted to you unconditionally.

YOUR BOLOGNESE SHOPPING LIST

Just as expectant parents prepare a nursery for their baby, so should you ready your home for the arrival of your Bolognese pup. If you have the necessary puppy supplies purchased and in place before he comes home, it will ease the puppy's transition from the warmth and familiarity of his mom and littermates to the brand-new environment of his new home and human family. You will be too busy to stock up and prepare your house after your pup comes home, that's for sure! Imagine how a pup must feel upon being transported to a strange new place. It's up to you to comfort him and to let your little pup know that he is going to be happy with you.

FOOD AND WATER BOWLS

Your puppy will need separate bowls for his food and water. Stainless steel pans are generally often preferred to plastic bowls since they sterilize better and pups are less inclined to chew on the metal. Heavy-duty ceramic bowls are popular and sturdy too.

THE DOG CRATE

If you think that crates are tools of punishment and confinement for when a dog has misbehaved, think again. Most breeders and almost all trainers recommend a crate as the preferred house-training aid as well as for all-around puppy training and safety. Because dogs are natural den creatures that prefer cave-like environments, the benefits of crate use are many. The crate provides the puppy with his very own "safe house," a cozy place to sleep, take a break or seek comfort with a favorite toy; a travel aid to house your dog when on the road, at motels or at the vet's office; a training aid to help teach your puppy proper toileting habits; and

a place of solitude when non-dog people happen to drop by and don't want a lively puppy—or even a well-behaved adult dog—saying hello or begging for attention.

Crates come in several types, although the wire crate and the fiberglass airline-type crate are the most popular. Both are safe and your puppy will adjust to either one, so the choice is up to you. The wire crates offer better visibility for the pup as well as better ventilation. Many of the wire crates fold down for easy transport. The fiberglass crates, similar to those used by the airlines for animal transport, are sturdier and more den-like, but do not fold down and are less ventilated than wire crates; this can be problematic in hot weather. Some of the newer crates are made of heavy plastic mesh;

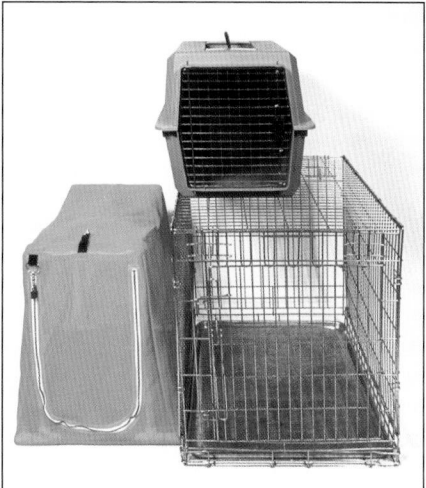

The three most popular types of crate: mesh on the left, wire on the right and fiberglass on top.

These littermates share a dental-care bone that helps clean their teeth as they chew.

these are very lightweight and fold up into slim-line suitcases. However, a mesh crate might not be suitable for a pup with manic chewing habits.

Your Bolognese will not need a large crate, but you should purchase a crate from the outset that will accommodate an adult Bolognese. Taking into consideration the adult's height at the shoulder of around 12 inches, purchase a crate that will allow the fully grown Bolognese to stand, lie down and turn around.

BEDDING AND CRATE PADS

Your puppy will enjoy some type of soft bedding in his "room" (the crate), something he can snuggle into and feel cozy and secure. Old towels or blankets are good choices for a young pup, since he may (and probably will) have a toileting accident or two in the crate or decide to chew on the bedding material. Once he is fully trained and out of the early

chewing stage, you can replace the puppy bedding with a permanent crate pad if you prefer. Crate pads and other dog beds run the gamut from inexpensive to high-end doggie-designer styles, but don't splurge on the good stuff until you are sure that your puppy is reliable and won't tear it up or make a mess on it.

PUPPY TOYS

Just as infants and children require objects to stimulate their minds and bodies, puppies need toys to entertain their curious brains, wiggly paws and achy teeth. A fun array of safe doggie toys will help satisfy your puppy's chewing instincts and distract him from gnawing on the leg of your antique chair or your new leather sofa. Most puppy toys

CRATE EXPECTATIONS

To make the crate more inviting to your puppy, you can offer his first meal or two inside the crate, always keeping the crate door open so that he does not feel confined. Keep a favorite toy or two in the crate for him to play with while inside. You can also cover the crate at night with a lightweight sheet to make it more den-like and remove the stimuli of household activity. Never put him into his crate as punishment or as you are scolding him, since he will then associate his crate with negative situations and avoid going there.

are cute and look as if they would be a lot of fun, but not all are necessarily safe or good for your puppy, so use caution when you go puppy-toy shopping.

Although Bolognese are not known to be voracious chewers like many other dogs, they still enjoy chewing. The best "chewci-fiers" are hard nylon and rubber bones, which are safe to gnaw on and come in sizes appropriate for all age groups and breeds. Be especially careful of raw or natural bones, which can splinter or develop dangerous sharp edges; pups can easily swallow or choke on those bone splinters. Veteri-narians often tell of surgical nightmares involving bits of splintered bone, because in addition to the danger of choking, the sharp pieces can damage the intestinal tract.

Similarly, rawhide chews, while a favorite of most dogs and puppies, can be equally dangerous. Pieces of rawhide are easily swallowed after they get soft and gummy from chewing, and dogs have been known to choke on pieces of ingested rawhide. Rawhide chews should be offered only when you can supervise the puppy.

Soft woolly toys are special puppy favorites. They come in a wide variety of cute shapes and sizes; some look like little stuffed animals. Puppies love to shake them up and toss them about or

TOYS 'R SAFE

The vast array of tantalizing puppy toys is staggering. Stroll through any pet-supply outlet and you will see that the choices can be overwhelming. However, not all dog toys are safe or sensible. Most very young puppies enjoy soft woolly toys that they can snuggle with and carry around. (You know they have outgrown them when they shred them up!) Avoid toys that have buttons, tabs or other enhancements that can be chewed off and swallowed. Soft toys that squeak are fun, but make sure your puppy does not disembowel the toy and remove (and swallow) the squeaker. Toys that rattle or make noise can excite a puppy, but they present the same danger as the squeaky kind and so require supervision. Hard rubber toys that bounce can also entertain a pup, but make sure that the toy is too big for your pup to swallow.

simply carry them around. Be careful of fuzzy toys that have button eyes or noses that your pup could chew off and swallow, and make sure that he does not "disembowel" a squeaky toy to remove the squeaker! Braided rope toys are similar in that they are fun to chew and toss around, but they shred easily and the strings are easy to swallow. The strings are not digestible and, if the puppy doesn't pass them in his stool, he could end up at the vet's office. As with rawhides, your puppy should be closely monitored with rope toys.

If you believe that your pup has ingested one of these forbidden objects, check his stool for the next couple of days to see if he passes them when he defecates. At the same time, also watch for signs of intestinal distress. A call to your veterinarian might be in order to get his advice and be on the safe side.

An all-time favorite toy for puppies (young and old!) is the

Check your pup's collar regularly for proper fit, remembering that both the pup and his beautiful coat grow quickly.

empty gallon milk jug. Hard plastic juice containers—46 ounces or more—are also excellent. Such containers make lots of noise when they are batted about and puppies go crazy with delight as they play with them. However, they don't often last very long, so be sure to remove and replace them when they get chewed up.

A word of caution about homemade toys: Be careful with your choices of non-traditional play objects. Never use old shoes or socks, since a puppy cannot distinguish between the old ones on which he's allowed to chew and the new ones in your closet that are strictly off limits. That principle applies to anything that resembles something that you don't want your puppy to chew.

COLLARS
A lightweight nylon collar is the best choice for a very young pup. Quick-click collars are easy to put on and remove, and they can be adjusted as the puppy grows. Introduce him to his collar as soon as he comes home to get him accustomed to wearing it. He'll get used to it quickly and won't mind a bit. Make sure that it is snug enough that it won't slip off yet loose enough to be comfortable for the pup. You should be able to slip two fingers between the collar and his neck. Check the collar often, as puppies grow in spurts and his collar can become too tight almost

overnight, especially considering that his coat grows more abundant as well. Choke collars are not appropriate for Bolognese as puppies or adults.

LEASHES

A 6-foot nylon lead is an excellent choice for a young puppy. It is lightweight and not as tempting to chew as a leather lead. You can switch to a 6-foot nylon lead after your pup has grown and is used to walking politely on a lead. For initial puppy walks and house-training purposes, you should invest in a shorter lead so that you have more control over the puppy. At first, you don't want him wandering too far away from you, and when taking him out for toileting you will want to keep him in the specific area chosen for his potty spot.

Once the puppy is heel-trained with a traditional leash, you can consider purchasing a retractable lead, which is excellent for walking adult dogs that are already leash-wise. This type of lead expands to allow the dog to roam farther away from you and explore a wider area when out walking and retracts when you need to keep him close to you.

HOME SAFETY FOR YOUR PUPPY

The importance of puppy-proofing cannot be overstated. In addition to making your house comfortable

TOXIC PLANTS
Plants are natural puppy magnets, but many can be harmful, even fatal, if ingested by a puppy or adult dog. Scout your yard and home interior and remove any plants, bushes or flowers that could be even mildly dangerous. It could save your puppy's life. You can obtain a complete list of toxic plants from your veterinarian, at the public library or by looking online.

for your Bolognese's arrival, you also must make sure that your house is safe for your puppy before you bring him home. There are countless hazards in the owner's personal living environment that a pup can sniff, chew, swallow or destroy. Many are obvious; others are not. Do a thorough advance house check to remove or rearrange those things that could hurt your puppy, keeping any potentially dangerous

A Dog-Safe Home

The dog-safety police are taking you on a house tour. Let's go room by room and see how safe your own home is for your new Bolognese. The following items are doggy dangers, so either they must be removed or the dog should be monitored or not allowed access to these areas.

Outdoors

- swimming pool
- pesticides
- toxic plants
- lawn fertilizers

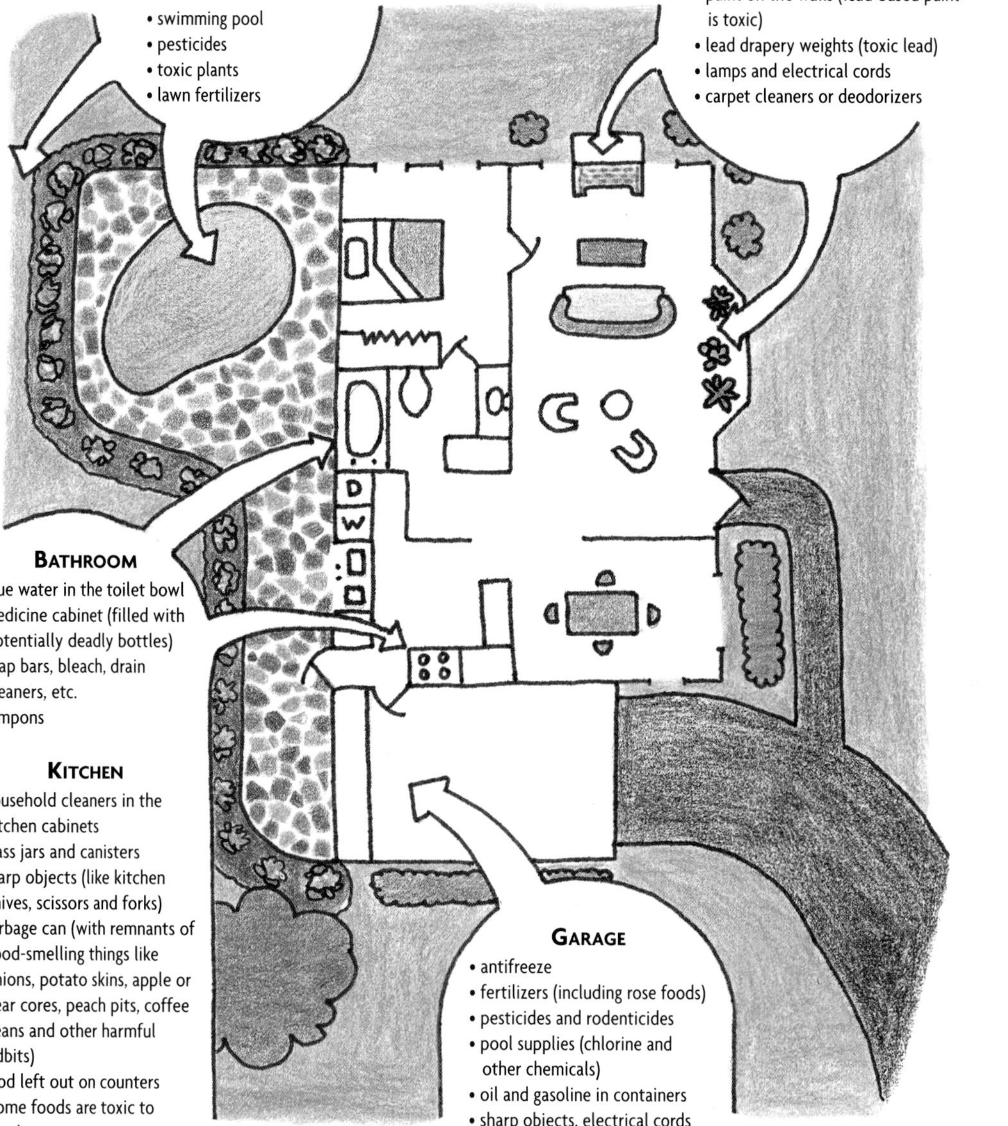

Living Room

- house plants (some varieties are poisonous)
- fireplace or wood-burning stove
- paint on the walls (lead-based paint is toxic)
- lead drapery weights (toxic lead)
- lamps and electrical cords
- carpet cleaners or deodorizers

Bathroom

- blue water in the toilet bowl
- medicine cabinet (filled with potentially deadly bottles)
- soap bars, bleach, drain cleaners, etc.
- tampons

Kitchen

- household cleaners in the kitchen cabinets
- glass jars and canisters
- sharp objects (like kitchen knives, scissors and forks)
- garbage can (with remnants of good-smelling things like onions, potato skins, apple or pear cores, peach pits, coffee beans and other harmful tidbits)
- food left out on counters (some foods are toxic to dogs)

Garage

- antifreeze
- fertilizers (including rose foods)
- pesticides and rodenticides
- pool supplies (chlorine and other chemicals)
- oil and gasoline in containers
- sharp objects, electrical cords and power tools

items out of areas to which he will have access.

Electrical cords are especially dangerous, since puppies view them as irresistible chew toys. Unplug and remove all exposed cords or fasten them beneath baseboards where the puppy cannot reach them. Veterinarians and firefighters can tell you horror stories about electrical burns and house fires that originated from puppy-chewed electrical cords. Consider this a most serious precaution for your puppy and the rest of your family.

Scout your home for tiny objects that might be seen at a pup's eye level. Keep medication bottles and cleaning supplies well out of reach, and do the same with waste baskets and other trash containers. It goes without saying that you should not use rodent poison or other toxic chemicals in any puppy area and that you must keep such containers safely locked up. You will be amazed at how many places a curious puppy can discover!

Once your house has cleared inspection, check your yard. A sturdy fence, well embedded into the ground, will give your dog a safe place to play and potty. Bolognese are not known to be climbers or fence jumpers, so a 5- to 6-foot-high fence should be adequate to contain an agile youngster or adult. Check the fence periodically for necessary

repairs. If there is a weak link or space to squeeze through, you can be sure that a determined Bolognese will discover it.

The garage and shed can be hazardous places for a pup, as things like fertilizers, chemicals and tools are usually kept there. It's best to keep these areas off limits to the pup. Antifreeze is especially dangerous to dogs, as they find the taste appealing and it only takes a few licks from the driveway to kill a dog, puppy or adult, small breed or large.

VISITING THE VETERINARIAN
A good veterinarian is your Bolognese puppy's best health-insurance policy. If you do not already have a vet, ask friends and experienced dog people in your area for recommendations so that you can select a vet with experience in small breeds before you

PUPPY PARASITES
Parasites are nasty little critters that live in or on your dog or puppy. Most puppies are born with ascarid roundworms, which are acquired from dormant ascarids residing in the dam. Other parasites can be acquired through contact with infected fecal matter. Take a stool sample to your vet for testing. He will prescribe a safe wormer to treat any parasites found in your puppy's stool. Always have a fecal test performed at your puppy's annual veterinary exam.

bring your Bolognese puppy home. Also arrange for your puppy's first veterinary examination beforehand, since many vets do not have appointments available immediately and your puppy should visit the vet within a day or so of coming home.

It's important to make sure your puppy's first visit to the vet is a pleasant and positive one. The vet should take great care to befriend the pup and handle him gently to make their first meeting a positive experience. The vet will give the pup a thorough physical examination and set up a schedule for vaccinations and other necessary wellness visits. Be sure to show your vet any health and inoculation records, which you should have received from your breeder. Your vet is a great source of canine health informa-

tion, so be sure to ask questions and take notes. Creating a health journal for your puppy will make a handy reference for his wellness and any future health problems that may arise.

MEETING THE FAMILY
Your Bolognese's homecoming is an exciting time for all members of the family, and it's only natural that everyone will be eager to meet him, pet him and play with him. However, for the puppy's sake, it's best to make these initial family meetings as uneventful as possible so that the pup is not overwhelmed with too much too soon. Remember, he has just left his dam and his littermates and is away from the breeder's home for the first time. Despite his fuzzy wagging tail, he is still apprehensive and

Meeting the family means the four-legged members, too. Take your time with new pet introductions, and supervise them as their friendship develops.

wondering where he is and who all these strange humans are. It's best to let him explore on his own and meet the family members as he feels comfortable. Let him investigate all the new smells, sights and sounds at his own pace. Children should be especially careful to not get overly excited, use loud voices or hug the pup too tightly. Be calm, gentle and affectionate, and be ready to comfort him if he appears frightened or uneasy.

Be sure to show your puppy his new crate during this first day home. Toss a treat or two inside the crate; if he associates the crate with food, he will associate the crate with good things. If he is comfortable with the crate, you can offer him his first meal inside it. Leave the door ajar so he can wander in and out as he chooses.

FIRST NIGHT IN HIS NEW HOME

So much has happened in your Bolognese puppy's first day away from the breeder. He's had his first car ride to his new home. He's met his new human family and perhaps the other family pets. He has explored his new house and yard, at least those places where he is to be allowed during his first weeks at home. He may have visited his new veterinarian. He has eaten his first meal or two away from his dam and litter-mates. Surely that's enough to tire

out a baby Bolognese pup—or so you hope!

It's bedtime. During the day, the pup investigated his crate, which is his new den and sleeping space, so it is not entirely strange to him. Line the crate with a soft towel or blanket that he can snuggle into and gently place him in the crate for the night. Some breeders send home a piece of bedding from where the pup slept with his littermates, and those familiar scents are a great comfort for the puppy on his first night without his siblings.

He will probably whine or cry. The puppy is objecting to the confinement and the fact that he is alone for the first time. This can be a stressful time for you as well as for the pup. It's important that you remain strong and don't let the puppy out of his crate to comfort him. He will fall asleep eventually. If you release him, the puppy will learn that crying

A pooped pup! Remember that your puppy is just a baby and needs plenty of time to rest.

means "out" and will continue that habit. You are laying the groundwork for future habits. Some breeders find that soft music can soothe a crying pup and help him get to sleep.

SOCIALIZING YOUR PUPPY
The first 20 weeks of your Bolognese puppy's life are the most important of his entire lifetime. A properly socialized puppy will grow up to be a confident and stable adult who will be a pleasure to live with and a welcome addition to the neighborhood.

The importance of socialization cannot be overemphasized. Research on canine behavior has proven that puppies who are not exposed to new sights, sounds, people and animals during their first 20 weeks of life will grow up to be timid and fearful, even aggressive, and unable to flourish outside of their home environment.

Socializing your puppy is not difficult and, in fact, will be a fun time for you both. Lead training goes hand in hand with socialization, so your puppy will be learning how to walk on a lead at the same time that he's meeting their neighborhood. Because the Bolognese is such a fascinating breed, everyone will enjoy meeting "the new kid on the block." Take him for short walks to the park and to other dog-

THE FAMILY TREE
Your puppy's pedigree is his family tree. Just as a child may resemble his parents and grandparents, so too will a puppy reflect the qualities, good and bad, of his ancestors, especially those in the first two generations. Therefore it's important to know as much as possible about a puppy's immediate relatives. Reputable and experienced breeders should be able to explain the pedigree and why they chose to breed from the particular dogs they used.

friendly places where he will encounter new people, especially children. Puppies automatically recognize children as "little people" and are drawn to play with them. Just make sure that you supervise these meetings and that the children do not get too rough or encourage him to play too hard. An overzealous pup can often nip too hard, frightening the child and in turn making the puppy overly excited. A bad experience in puppyhood can impact a dog for life; thus a pup that has a negative experience with a child may grow up to be shy or even aggressive around children.

Take your puppy along on your daily errands. Puppies are natural "people magnets" and most people who see your pup will want to pet him. All of these encounters will help to mold him into a confident adult dog.

Likewise, you will soon feel like a confident, responsible dog owner, rightly proud of your mannerly Bolognese.

The eight-to-ten-week-old period is also known as the "fear period." This is a serious imprinting period, and all contact during this time should be gentle and positive. A frightening or negative event could leave a permanent impression that could affect his future behavior if a similar situation arises. Most Bolognese breeders do not release puppies to new homes until 10–12 weeks of age, so your pup should still be with the breeder during this fear period.

Make sure that your puppy has received his first and second rounds of vaccinations before you expose him to other dogs or bring him to places that other dogs may frequent. Avoid dog parks and other strange-dog areas until your vet assures you that your puppy is fully immunized and resistant to the diseases that can be passed between canines. Discuss safe early socialization with your breeder, as some breeders recommend socializing the puppy even before he has received all his inoculations, depending on the individual pup.

LEADER OF THE PUPPY'S PACK
Like other canines, your puppy needs an authority figure, someone he can look up to and regard as the leader of his "pack." His first pack leader was his dam, who taught him to be polite and not chew too hard on her ears or nip at her muzzle. He learned those same lessons from his littermates. If he played too rough, they cried in pain and stopped the game, which sent an important message to the rowdy puppy.

As puppies play together, they are also struggling to determine who will be the boss. Being pack animals, dogs need someone to be in charge. If a litter of puppies remained together beyond puppyhood, one of the pups would emerge as the strongest one, the one who calls the shots.

Once your puppy leaves the pack, he will look intuitively for a new leader. If he does not recognize you as that leader, he will try to assume that position

Bolognese littermates play, eat, sleep and learn together, forming a bond as part of their puppy pack.

for himself. Of course, it is hard to imagine your adorable Bolognese puppy trying to be in charge when he is so small and seemingly helpless. You must remember that these are natural canine instincts. Do not cave in and allow your pup to get the upper "paw!"

Just as socialization is so important during these first 20 weeks, so too is your puppy's early education. He was born without any bad habits. He does not know what is good or bad behavior. If he does things like nipping and digging, it's because he is having fun and doesn't know that humans consider these things as "bad." It's your job to teach him proper puppy manners, and this is the best time to accomplish that—before he has developed bad habits, since it is much more difficult to "unlearn" or correct unacceptable learned behavior than to teach good behavior from the start.

Make sure that all members of the family understand the importance of being consistent when training their new puppy. If you tell the puppy to stay off the sofa and your daughter allows him to cuddle on the couch to watch her favorite television show, your pup will be confused about what he is and is not allowed to do. Have a family conference before your pup comes home so that everyone understands the basic principles of puppy training and the rules you have set forth for the pup and agrees to follow them.

The old adage "an ounce of prevention is worth a pound of cure" is especially true when it comes to puppies. It is much easier to prevent inappropriate behavior than it is to change it. It's also easier and less stressful for the pup, since it will keep discipline to a minimum and create a more positive learning environment for him. That, in turn, will also be easier on you.

Here are a few commonsense tips to keep your belongings safe and your puppy out of trouble:

• Keep your closet doors closed and your shoes, socks and other apparel off the floor so your puppy can't get at them.
• Keep a secure lid on the trash container or put the trash where your puppy can't dig into it. He can't damage what he can't reach!
• Supervise your puppy at all times to make sure he is not getting into mischief. If he starts to chew the corner of the rug, you can distract him instantly by tossing a toy for him to fetch. You also will be able to whisk him outside when you notice that he is about to piddle on the carpet. If you can't see your puppy, you can't teach him or correct his behavior.

TEETHING TIME

All puppies chew. It's normal canine behavior. Chewing just plain feels good to a puppy, especially during the three- to five-month teething period when the adult teeth are breaking through the gums. Rather than attempting to eliminate such a strong natural chewing instinct, you will be more successful if you redirect it and teach your puppy what he may or may not chew. Correct inappropriate chewing with a sharp "No!" and offer him a chew toy, praising him when he takes it. Don't become discouraged. Chewing usually decreases after the adult teeth have come in.

SOLVING PUPPY PROBLEMS

CHEWING AND NIPPING

Nipping at fingers and toes is normal puppy behavior. Chewing is also the way that puppies investigate their surroundings. However, you will have to teach your puppy that chewing anything other than his toys is not acceptable. That won't happen overnight and, at times, puppy teeth will test your patience. However, if you allow nipping and chewing to continue, he will develop into an adult with a bad chewing habit.

Whenever your puppy nips your hand or fingers, cry out "Ouch!" in a loud voice, which should startle your puppy and stop him from nipping, even if only for a moment. Immediately distract him by offering a small treat or an appropriate toy for him to chew instead (which means having chew toys and puppy treats handy or in your pockets at all times). Praise him when he takes the toy and tell him what a good fellow he is. Praise is just as, or even more, important to puppy training as discipline and correction.

Puppies also tend to nip at children more often than adults, since they perceive little ones to be more vulnerable and more similar to their littermates. Teach your children appropriate responses to nipping behavior and, if they are unable to handle it themselves, you may have to intervene. Puppy nips can be quite painful and a child's frightened reaction will only encourage

A curious pup with a need to chew will find that most anything gets the job done.

A few toys, but not too many so as to overwhelm him, will keep a pup interested and occupied.

A few toys, but not too many so as to overwhelm him, will keep a pup interested and occupied.

a puppy to nip harder, which is a natural canine response. As with all other puppy situations, interaction between your Bolognese puppy and children should be supervised.

Chewing on objects, not just family members' fingers and ankles, is also normal canine behavior that can be especially tedious (for the owner, not the pup) during the teething period when the puppy's adult teeth are coming in. At this stage, chewing just plain feels good. Furniture legs and cabinet corners are common puppy favorites. Shoes and other personal items also taste pretty good to a pup.

The best solution is, once again, prevention. If you value something, keep it tucked away and out of reach. You can't hide your dining-room table in a closet, but you can try to deflect the chewing by applying a bitter product made just to deter dogs from chewing. This spray-on substance is vile-tasting, although safe for dogs, and most puppies will avoid the forbidden object after one tiny taste. You also can apply the product to your leather leash if the puppy tries to chew on his lead during leash-training sessions.

Keep a ready supply of safe chews handy to offer your Bolognese as a distraction when he starts to chew on something that's a "no-no." Remember, at this tender age he does not yet know what is permitted or forbidden, so you have to be "on call" every minute he's awake and on the prowl.

You may lose a treasure or two during puppy's growing-up period, and the furniture could sustain a nasty nick or two. These can be trying times, so be prepared for those inevitable accidents and comfort yourself in knowing that this too shall pass.

PUPPY WHINING

Puppies often cry and whine, just as infants and little children do. It's their way of telling us that they are lonely or in need of attention. Your puppy will miss his littermates and will feel insecure when he is left alone. You may be out of the house or just in another room, but he will still feel alone. During these times, the puppy's crate should be his personal comfort station, a place all his own where he can feel safe and secure. Once he learns that being alone is okay and not something to be feared, he will settle down without crying or objecting. You might want to leave a radio on while he is crated, as the sound of human voices can be soothing and will give the impression that people are around.

Give your puppy a favorite cuddly toy or chew toy to entertain him whenever he is crated. You will both be happier: the puppy because he is safe in his den, and you because he is

quiet, safe and not getting into puppy escapades that can wreak havoc in your house or cause him danger.

To make sure that your puppy will always view his crate as a safe and cozy place, never, *ever* use the crate as punishment. That's the best way to turn the crate into a negative place that the pup will want to avoid. Sure, you can use the crate for your own peace of mind if puppy is getting into trouble and needs some "time out." Just don't let him know that! Never scold the pup and immediately place him in the crate. Count to ten, give him a couple of hugs and maybe a treat, then scoot him into his crate.

It's also important not to make a big fuss when he is released from the crate. That will make getting out of the crate more

It's a big world for a small pup— will you be a worthy guardian and caregiver?

appealing than being in the crate, which is just the opposite of what you are trying to achieve.

FOOD GUARDING

Some dogs are picky eaters; others seem to inhale their food without chewing it. Occasionally the true "chow hound" will become protective of his food, which is one dangerous step toward other aggressive behavior. Food guarding is obvious—your puppy will growl, snarl or even attempt to bite you if you approach his food bowl or put your hand into his bowl while he's eating.

This behavior is not acceptable and very preventable! If your puppy is an especially voracious eater, sit next to him occasionally while he eats and dangle your fingers in his food bowl. Don't feed him in a corner, where he could feel possessive of his eating space. Rather, place his food bowl in an open area of your kitchen where you are in close proximity. Occasionally remove his food in mid-meal, tell him he's a good boy and return his bowl.

If your pup becomes possessive of his food, look for other signs of future aggression, like guarding his favorite toys or refusing to obey obedience commands that he knows. Consult an obedience trainer for help in reinforcing obedience so your Bolognese will fully understand that you are the boss.

DOMESTIC SQUABBLES

How well your new Bolognese will get along with your older dog who has squatter's rights depends largely on the individual dogs. Like people, some dogs are more gregarious than others and will enjoy having a furry friend to play with. Others will not be thrilled at the prospect of sharing their dog space with another canine.

It's best to introduce the dogs to each other on neutral ground, away from home, so the resident dog won't feel so possessive. Keep both puppy and adult on loose leads (loose is very important, as a tight lead sends negative signals and can intimidate either dog) and allow them to sniff and do their doggie things. A few raised hackles are normal, with the older dog pawing at the youngster. Let the two work things out between them unless you see signs of real aggression, such as deep growls or curled lips and serious snarls. You may have to keep them separated until the veteran gets used to the new family member, often after the pup

Interaction between your Bolognese and other pets must be supervised to assure that all members of the household get along.

has outgrown the silly puppy stage and is more mature in stature. Take precautions to make sure that the puppy does not become frightened by the older dog's behavior.

Whatever happens, it's important to make your resident dog feel secure. (Jealousy is normal among dogs, too!) Pay extra attention to the older dog: feed him first, hug him first and don't insist he share his toys or space with the new pup until he's ready. If the two are still at odds months later, consult an obedience professional for advice.

Cat introductions are easier, believe it or not. Being agile and independent creatures, cats will scoot to high places, out of puppy's reach. A cat might even tease the puppy and cuff him from above when the pup comes within paw's reach. However, most will end up buddies if you just let dog-and-cat nature run its course.

WATCH THE WATER

To help your puppy sleep through the night without having to relieve himself, remove his water bowl after 7 P.M. Offer him a couple of ice cubes during the evening to quench his thirst. Never leave water in a puppy's crate, as this is inviting puddles of mishaps.

PROPER CARE OF YOUR

BOLOGNESE

Adding a Bolognese to your household means adding a new family member who will need your care each and every day. When your Bolognese pup first comes home, you will start a routine with him so that, as he grows up, your dog will have a daily schedule just as you do. The aspects of your dog's daily care will likewise become regular parts of your day, so you'll both have a new schedule. Dogs learn by consistency and they thrive on routine: regular times for meals, exercise, grooming and potty trips are just as important for your dog as they are for you! Your dog's

At two days old, these pups' only food is their mother's milk, providing them with the nutrition and immunity that they need at this tender age.

schedule will depend much on your family's daily routine, but remember, you now have a new member of the family who is part of your day, every day.

FEEDING
Feeding your dog the best diet is based on various factors, including age, activity level, overall condition and size of breed. When you visit the breeder, he will share with you his advice about the proper diet for your dog based on his experience with the breed and the foods with which he has had success. Likewise, your vet will be a helpful source of advice throughout the dog's life and will aid you in planning a diet for optimal health.

FEEDING THE PUPPY
Of course, your pup's very first food will be his dam's milk. There may be special situations in which pups fail to nurse, necessitating that the breeder hand-feeds them with a formula, but, for the most part, pups spend the first weeks of life nursing from their dam. The breeder weans the pups by gradually introducing solid foods

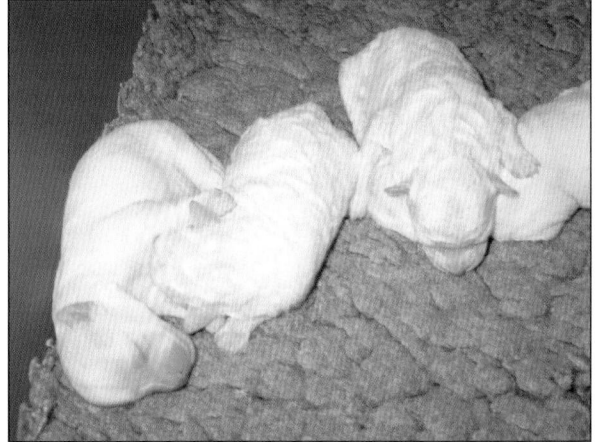

and decreasing the milk meals. Pups may even start themselves off on the weaning process, albeit inadvertently, if they snatch bites from their mom's food bowl.

By the time the pups are ready for new homes, they are fully weaned and eating a good puppy food. As a new owner, you may be thinking, "Great! The breeder has taken care of the hard part!" Not so fast.

A puppy's first year of life is the time when all, or most, of his growth and development takes place. This is a delicate time, and diet plays a huge role in proper skeletal and muscular formation. Improper diet and exercise habits can lead to damaging problems that will compromise the dog's health and movement for his entire life. That being said, new owners should not worry needlessly. With the myriad types of food formulated specifically for growing pups of different-sized breeds, dog-food manufacturers have taken much of the guesswork out of feeding your puppy well. Since growth-food formulas are designed to provide the nutrition that a growing puppy needs, it is unnecessary and, in fact, can prove harmful to add supplements to the diet. Research has shown that too much of certain vitamins and minerals predisposes a dog to skeletal problems. It's by no means a case of "if a little is good,

VARIETY IS THE SPICE

Although dog-food manufacturers contend that dogs don't like variety in their diets, studies show quite the opposite to be true. Dogs would much rather vary their meals than eat the same old chow day in and day out. Dry kibble is no more exciting for a dog than the same bowl of bran flakes would be for you. Fortunately, there are dozens of varieties available on the market, and your dog will likely show a preference for certain flavors over others. A word of warning: don't overdo it or you'll develop a fussy eater who only prefers chopped beef fillet and asparagus tips every night.

a lot is better!" At every stage of your dog's life, too much or too little in the way of nutrients can be harmful, which is why a manufactured complete food is the easiest way to know that your dog is getting what he needs.

Because of a young pup's small body and accordingly small digestive system, his daily portion will be divided up into small meals throughout the day. This can mean starting off with three or more meals a day and decreasing the number of meals as the pup matures. For the adult, dividing the day's food into two meals on a morning/evening schedule is healthier for the dog's digestion than one large daily portion.

These two-week old pups will get all the nutrition they need from their mother's milk.

Regarding the feeding schedule, feeding the pup at the same times and in the same place each day is important, both for housebreaking purposes and for establishing the dog's everyday routine. As for the amount to feed, growing puppies generally need proportionately more food per body weight than their adult counterparts, but a pup should never be allowed to gain excess weight. Dogs of all ages should be kept in proper body condition, but extra weight can strain a pup's developing frame, causing skeletal problems.

Watch your pup's weight as he grows and, if the recommended amounts seem to be too much or too little for your pup, consult the vet about appropriate dietary changes. Keep in mind that treats, although small, can quickly add up throughout the day, contributing unnecessary calories.

Treats are fine when used prudently; opt for dog treats specially formulated to be healthy or nutritious snacks like small pieces of cheese or cooked chicken.

FEEDING THE ADULT DOG

For the adult (meaning physically mature) dog, feeding properly is about maintenance, not growth. Again, correct weight is a concern. Your dog should appear fit and should have an evident "waist." His ribs should not be protruding (a sign of being underweight), but they should be covered by only a slight layer of fat. Under normal circumstances, an adult dog can be maintained fairly easily with a good, nutritionally complete adult-formula food.

Factor treats into your dog's overall daily caloric intake, and avoid offering table scraps. Not only are certain "people foods," like chocolate, nuts, grapes, raisins, onions and quantities of garlic, toxic to dogs, but feeding from your plate also encourages begging and overeating. Overweight dogs are more prone to health problems. Research has even shown that obesity takes years off a dog's life. With that in

DIET DON'TS

- Got milk? Don't give it to your dog! Dogs cannot tolerate large quantities of cows' milk, as they do not have the enzymes to digest lactose.
- You may have heard of dog owners who add raw eggs to their dogs' food for a shiny coat or to make the food more palatable, but consumption of raw eggs too often can cause a deficiency of the vitamin biotin.
- Avoid feeding table scraps, as they will upset the balance of the dog's complete food. Additionally, fatty or highly seasoned foods can cause upset canine stomachs.
- Do not offer raw meat to your dog. Raw meat can contain parasites; it also is high in fat.
- Vitamin A toxicity in dogs can be caused by too much raw liver, especially if the dog already gets enough vitamin A in his balanced diet, which should be the case.
- Bones like chicken, pork chop and other soft bones are not suitable, as they easily splinter.

mind, resist the urge to overfeed and over-treat, remembering that calories add up quickly in small dogs. Don't make unnecessary additions to your dog's diet, whether with tidbits or with extra vitamins and minerals.

The amount of food needed for proper maintenance will vary depending on the individual dog's activity level, but you will be able to tell if the daily portions are keeping him in good shape. With the wide variety of good complete foods available, choosing what to feed is largely a matter of personal preference. Just as with the puppy, the adult dog should have consistency in his mealtimes and feeding place.

The breeder starts the pup on solid food as part of the weaning process.

A dinner date with a littermate!

What does aging have to do with your dog's diet? No, he won't get a discount at the local diner's early-bird special. Yes, he will require some dietary changes to accommodate the changes that come along with increased age. One change is that the older dog's dietary needs become more similar to that of a puppy. Specifically, dogs can metabolize more protein as youngsters and seniors than in the adult-maintenance stage. Discuss with your vet whether you need to switch to a higher protein or senior-formulated food or if your current adult-dog food contains sufficient nutrition for the senior.

In addition to a consistent routine, regular mealtimes also allow you to see how much your dog is eating. If the dog seems never to be satisfied or, likewise, becomes uninterested in his food, you will know right away that something is wrong and can consult the vet.

DIETS FOR THE AGING DOG

In the Bolognese, the average life expectancy is 12–14 years. A good rule of thumb is that once a dog has reached 75% of his expected lifespan, he has reached "senior citizen" or geriatric status. Using this calculation, a Bolognese will be considered a senior at around age nine, though a senior health-care program and dietary changes may be suggested earlier by your vet. Fortunately for Bolognese owners, small breeds tend to have the longest lifespans among dogs.

NOT HUNGRY?

No dog in his right mind would turn down his dinner, would he? If you notice that your dog has lost interest in his food, there could be any number of causes. Dental problems are a common cause of appetite loss, one that is often overlooked. If your dog has a toothache, a loose tooth or sore gums from infection, chances are it doesn't feel so good to chew. Think about when you've had a toothache! If your dog does not approach the food bowl with his usual enthusiasm, look inside his mouth for signs of a problem. Whatever the cause, you'll want to consult your vet so that your chow hound can get back to his happy, hungry self as soon as possible.

Watching the dog's weight remains essential, even more so in the senior stage. Older dogs are already more vulnerable to illness, and obesity only contributes to his susceptibility to problems. As the older dog becomes less active and thus exercises less, his regular portions may cause him to gain weight. At this point, you may consider decreasing his daily food intake or switching to a reduced-calorie food. As with other changes, you should consult your vet for advice.

TYPES OF FOOD AND READING THE LABEL

When selecting the type of food to feed your dog, it is important to check the label and read the ingredients. Many dry-food products have soybean, corn or rice as the main ingredient. The main ingredient will be listed first on the label, with the rest of the ingredients following in descending order according to their proportion in the food. While these types of dry food are fine, you should look into dry foods based on meat or fish. These are better-quality foods and thus higher priced. However, they may be just as economical in the long run, because studies have shown that it takes a lesser quantity of the higher quality foods to maintain a dog.

Comparing the various types of manufactured dog foods, dry,

QUENCHING HIS THIRST

Is your dog drinking more than normal and trying to lap up everything in sight? Excessive drinking has many different causes. Obvious causes for a dog's being thirstier than usual are hot weather and vigorous exercise. However, if your dog is drinking more for no apparent reason, you could have cause for concern. Serious conditions like kidney or liver disease, diabetes and various types of hormonal problems can all be indicated by excessive drinking. If you notice your dog's being excessively thirsty, contact your vet at once. Hopefully there will be a simpler explanation, but the earlier a serious problem is detected, the sooner it can be treated, with a better rate of cure.

canned and semi-moist, dry foods contain the least amount of water whereas canned foods contain the most water. Proportionately, dry foods are the most calorie- and nutrient-dense, which means that you need more of a canned food product to supply the same amount of nutrition. For large dogs, this can be an issue! Small breeds, however, do fine on canned foods and, if feeding dry food to a small dog, it is wise to choose a "small bite" formula with pieces that are easier for their small mouths and teeth to handle. You may find success mixing the food types as well.

A well-balanced dog food along with regular exercise with playmates—human or canine—will keep your Bolognese in great shape.

Water is important for all dogs but even more so for those fed dry foods, as there is no high water content in their food.

There are strict controls that regulate the nutritional content of dog food, and a food has to meet the minimum requirements in order to be considered "complete and balanced." It is important that you choose such a food for your dog, so check the label to be sure that your chosen food meets the requirements. If not, look for a food that clearly states on the label that it is formulated to be complete and balanced for your dog's particular stage of life.

Recommendations for amounts to feed will also be indicated on the label. You should also ask your vet about proper food portions, and you will keep an eye on your dog's condition to see if the recommended amounts are adequate. If he becomes over-

or underweight, you will need to make adjustments and this also would be a good time to consult your vet.

The food label may also make feeding suggestions, such as if moistening a dry-food product is recommended. Sometimes a splash of water will make the food more palatable for the dog and even enhance the flavor; it may also slow down an especially enthusiastic eater. Don't be overwhelmed by the many factors that go into feeding your dog. Manufacturers of complete and balanced foods make it easy, and once you find the right food and amounts for your own dog, his daily feeding will be a matter of routine.

DON'T FORGET THE WATER!
For a dog, it's always time for a drink! Regardless of what type of food he eats, there's no debate that he needs plenty of water. Fresh cold water, in a clean bowl, should be freely available to your dog at all times. There are special circumstances, such as during puppy housebreaking, when you will want to monitor your pup's water intake so that you will be able to predict when he will need to relieve himself, but water must be available to him nonetheless. Water is essential for hydration and proper body function just as it is in humans.

You will get to know how much your dog typically drinks in

a day. Of course, in the heat or if exercising vigorously, he will be more thirsty and will drink more. However, if he begins to drink noticeably more water for no apparent reason, this could signal any of various problems and you are advised to consult your vet.

Water is the best drink for dogs. Some owners are tempted to give milk from time to time or to moisten dry food with milk, but dogs do not have the enzymes necessary to digest the lactose in milk, which is much different than the milk that nursing puppies receive. Therefore, stick

with clean fresh water to quench your dog's thirst, and always have it readily available to him.

The Bolognese is a sturdy little dog— he enjoys doing things with you and will be sure to let you know when he needs a break.

KEEP OFF THE GRASS

As a conscientious dog owner, you never use fertilizers, pesticides or other harmful landscaping chemicals. However, you cannot expect everyone in your neighborhood to do the same. When out walking your dog, it is best to stay on sidewalks and not to allow your dog to explore the neighbors' front lawns; of course, this is for your dog's safety as well as for maintaining good rapport with the neighbors. Highly tailored yards are danger zones, and many (but not all) lawn services put up signs or flags to warn others of recently treated grass. Dogs can absorb these chemicals through their feet or ingest them if they lick their paws following walks. To be on the safe side, rinse or wipe down your dog's feet each time you come in from a walk.

EXERCISE

We all know the importance of exercise for humans, so it should come as no surprise that it is essential for our canine friends as well. Now, regardless of your own level of fitness, get ready to assume the role of personal trainer for your dog. It's not as hard as it sounds, and it will have health benefits for you, too.

Just as with anything you do with your dog, you must set a routine for his exercise. It's the same as your going on a run each morning before work or never missing the 7 P.M. aerobics class. If you plan it and get into the habit of actually doing it, it will become just another part of your day. Think of it as making daily exercise appointments with your dog, and stick to your schedule.

As a rule, dogs in normal health should have at least a half-hour of activity each day. Dogs with health or orthopedic problems may have specific limitations and their exercise plans are best devised with the help of a vet. For healthy dogs, there are many ways to fit 30 minutes of activity into your day. Depending on your schedule, you may plan a 15-minute walk or activity session in the morning or again in the evening, or do it all at once in a half-hour session each day. Walking is the most popular way to exercise a dog (it's good for you, too!). While the breed does not have extensive exercise needs, he is a hardy little dog that can keep up with active owners. Bolognese enjoy time spent with their owners at play and at rest.

Some precautions should be taken with a puppy's exercise. During his first year, when he is growing and developing, he should not be subject to vigorous activity that stresses his body. Short walks at a comfortable pace and play sessions in the home and yard are good for a growing pup, and his exercise can be increased as he grows up.

For overweight dogs, dietary changes and activity will help the goal of weight loss (sound familiar?). While they should of course be encouraged to be active, remember not to overdo it as the excess weight is already putting

strain on their vital organs and bones.

Regardless of your dog's condition and activity level, exercise offers benefits to all dogs and owners. Consider the fact that dogs who are kept active are more stimulated both physically and mentally, meaning that they are less apt to become bored and lapse into destructive behavior. Also consider the benefits of one-on-one time with your dog every day, continually strengthening the bond between the two of you. Furthermore, exercising together will improve both of your health and longevity. Both of you need exercise, and now you both have a workout partner and motivator!

GROOMING
The Bolognese needs to be thoroughly combed and brushed at least three or four times a week. Pet shops offer a large selection of special combs and brushes suitable for the proper care of your Bolognese. Purchase a high-quality slicker brush. Do not purchase a cheap slicker brush, as it can damage your dog's skin and coat. Regular brushing and combing are necessary to prevent the coat from matting. Mats and tangles may form very quickly; if left unattended for just a few days, they will be impossible to eliminate with simple combing or brushing. Removing mats is

very painful for the dog, and the torn-out hair will hardly grow back. Regular care is therefore much more preferable.

If mats do form, scissors are not necessarily the only option. The affected patches of coat can be soaked with a conditioning lotion and the mats carefully plucked apart with your fingers. In the worst-case scenario, scissors are required to cut off the matted hair. This is then done according to the lie of the coat in order to prevent possible injury to the dog. Thereafter, loose hair is plucked and combed out.

It is necessary to accustom your Bolognese to the grooming routine when he is still a pup. A young dog that becomes accustomed to the caring hands of a human will remain easy to handle and willing throughout his life. Who would want every grooming session with his dog to be a struggle, even if the dog is small? The Bolognese is therefore acclimated to grooming and taught how to behave by using a verbal command. Choose a word that you will always use at grooming time, like "Pretty" or "Makeup." Use your word, then put your Bolognese on his grooming surface (a grooming table is preferable) and give him the command "Stand." A dog that is nervous on the grooming table, sits down over and over again, fidgets about continuously or

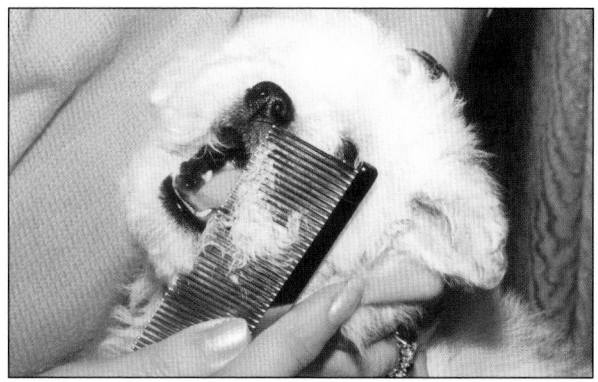

Be gentle with your puppy's grooming, especially in sensitive areas, as you don't want him to protest every time you get out the comb.

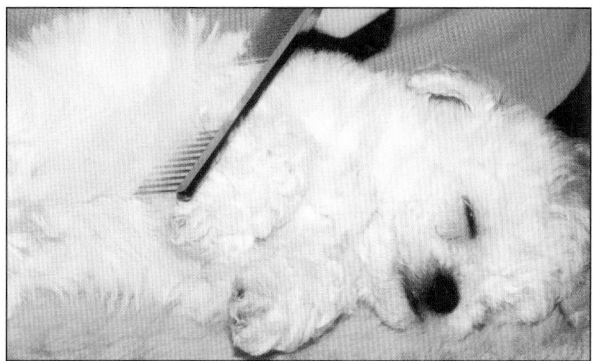

Laying the pup on his side makes him more comfortable while you tend to the hard-to-reach places like the "armpits."

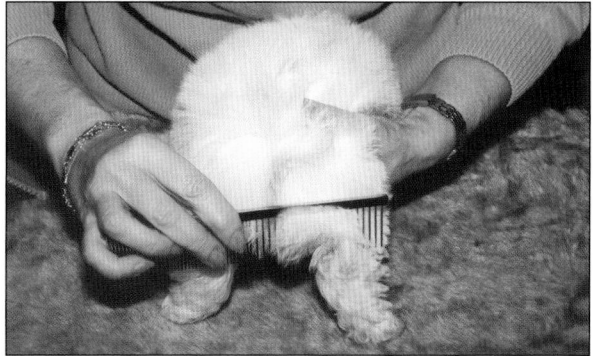

Groom the whole body, front to back, holding the puppy so that he is safe and secure on the grooming table.

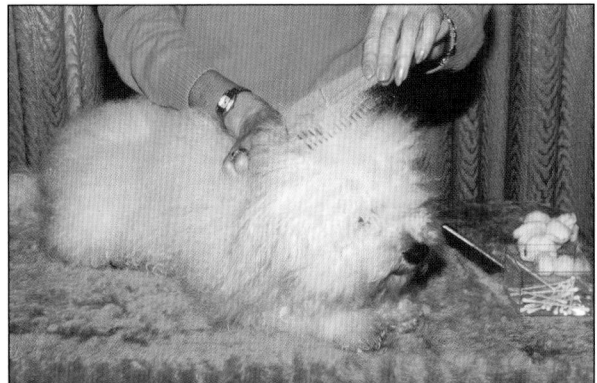

From head...

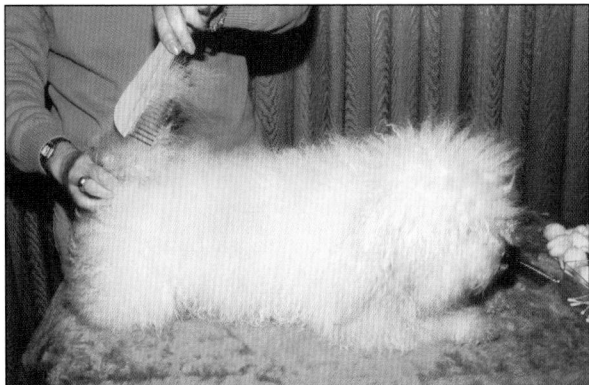

To tail...

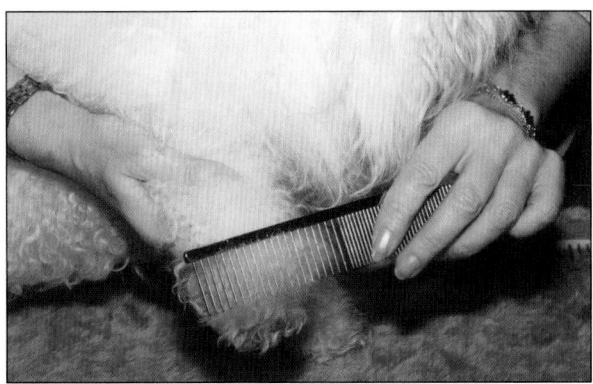

To toe...don't neglect any part of the body. Give your Bolognese a thorough all-over combing to prevent mats and tangles.

simply does not do what he is supposed to do is no fun to groom.

You need calm and obedient behavior from your Bolognese during grooming sessions. This may require enforcing the "stand" command by repetition and manual manipulation, an educational measure that should begin the first time he is groomed. When he is still a pup, you have to be careful to prevent him from jumping or falling off the table. He can easily injure himself from such a fall. This is best done by placing him sideways on the table in front of you, with his head pointing to your left (if you are right-handed). Using your left hand with the palm turned up, hold him between his forelegs from the front so that his chest is supported. If the little dog now begins to wriggle, you can control him easily, remind him to "stand" and bring him back into the right position.

Care has to be taken to really reach all parts of the body in order to prevent mats from forming and possibly spoiling the coat despite your efforts. Comb through with a metal comb specifically designed for mat-prevention by working it in layers from the belly upwards to the back, first on one side and then on the other, and then comb the tail from the tip to the base. Combing is done from the tips of the hair to the

SELECTING THE RIGHT BRUSHES AND COMBS

Will a rubber curry make my dog look slicker? Is a rake smaller than a pin brush? Do I choose nylon or natural bristles? Buying a dog brush can make the hairs on your head stand on end! Here's a quick once-over to educate you on the different types of brushes.

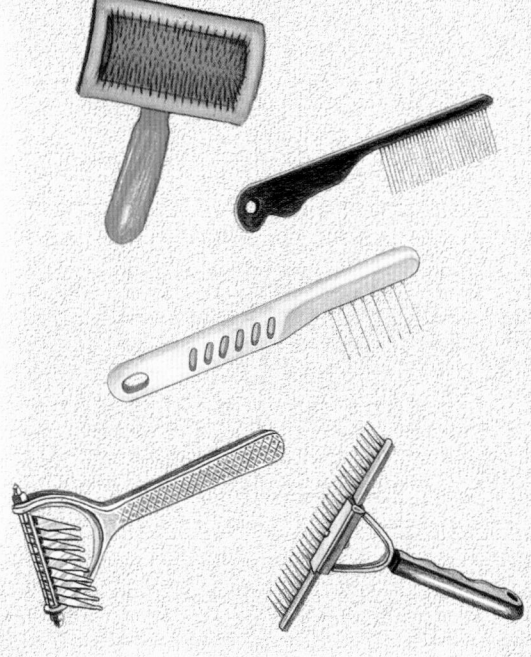

Slicker Brush: Fine metal prongs closely set on a curved base. Used to remove dead coat from the undercoat of medium- to long-coated breeds.

Pin Brush: Metal pins, often covered with rubber tips, set on an oval base. Used to remove shedding hair and is gentler than a slicker brush.

Metal Comb: Steel teeth attached to a steel handle; the closeness and size of the teeth vary greatly. A "flea comb" has tiny teeth set very closely together and is used to find fleas in a dog's coat. Combs with wider teeth are used for detangling longer coats.

Rake: Long-toothed comb with a short handle. Used to remove undercoat from heavily coated breeds with dense undercoats.

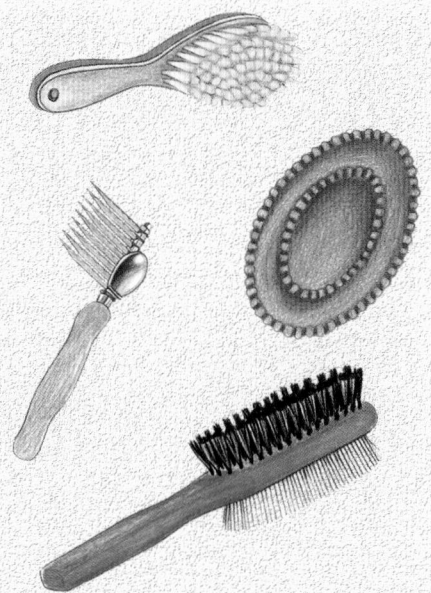

Soft-bristle Brush: Nylon or natural bristles set in a plastic or wood base. Used on short coats or long coats (without undercoats).

Rubber Curry: Rubber prongs, with or without a handle. Used for short-coated dogs. Good for use during shampooing.

Combination Brushes: Two-sided brush with a different type of bristle on each side; for example, pin brush on one side and slicker on the other, or bristle brush on one side and pin brush on the other. An economical choice if you need two kinds of brushes.

Grooming Glove: Sometimes called a hound glove; used to give sleek-coated dogs a once-over.

A shower spray or similar attachment will help you wet the coat thoroughly, all the way down to the skin.

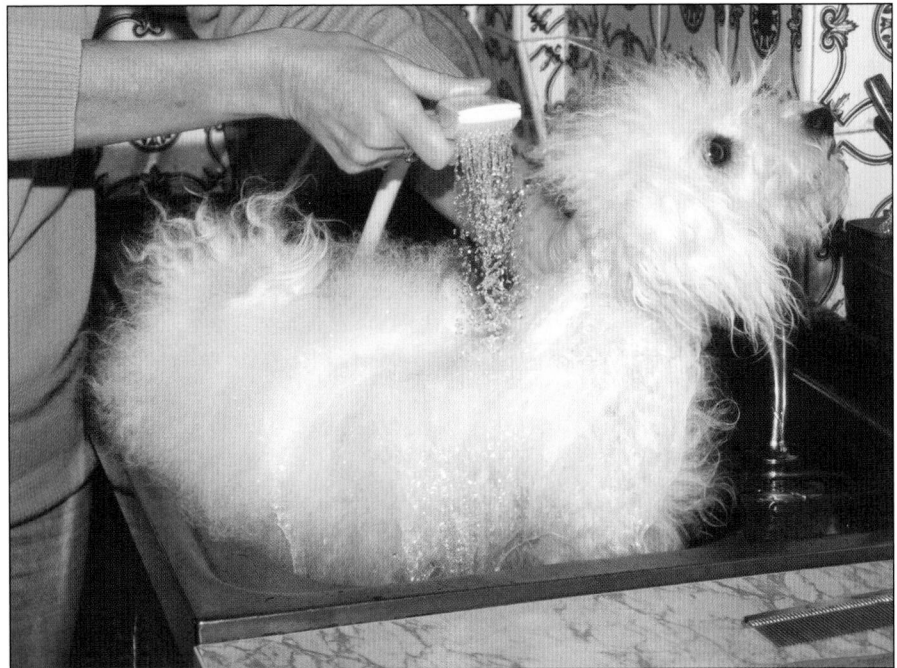

body, as otherwise too much of the precious covering hair may be lost—your Bolognese would look like a plucked chicken.

Once one side of the body has been finished, the dog is turned around so that his head now points in the opposite direction. Your left hand, which has been holding the dog in place, is now pushed through the hind legs so that your palm can support the belly. This enables you to work securely on the right side of the dog's body. While grooming, you should talk to your Bolognese in a pleasant and praising voice, telling him how beautiful he is and how much

you love him for being so obedient. Once the work on the body has been completed, the dog is made to sit facing you so that you can attend to the beard and head. Initially, this procedure may be quite stressful for both your agitated pup and you, but this is rather normal. It

NEVER CLIP A BOLOGNESE
You should never try to simplify your Bolognese's coat care by cutting the hair short. This would cause the dog to lose the protective cushion of air formed by the long coat that keeps him warm in winter and protects him from overheating in summer.

is just important that eventually the dog becomes used to standing obediently on the grooming table. It should not take long before he learns that nothing bad is going to happen to him there.

BATHING

Despite his white coat, bathing your Bolognese is actually necessary only if he is very dirty or in preparation for a show. Even after a walk through the woods or in bad weather, it usually suffices to wipe him down with a towel or just give him a rinse (without shampoo).

Bathing too frequently can have negative effects on the skin and coat, removing natural oils and causing dryness.

AN OCCASIONAL BATH

Bathing a dog too often destroys the natural protective layer of the skin, often resulting in dandruff and persistent itchiness. For the same reason, only a mild shampoo, specifically made for dogs, should be used.

If you give your dog his first bath when he is young, he will become accustomed to the process. Wrestling a dog into the tub or chasing a freshly shampooed dog who has escaped from the bath will be no fun! Most dogs don't naturally enjoy their baths, but you at least want yours to cooperate with you.

Use a blow dryer on low heat; dogs have sensitive skin, and high temperatures can also damage the coat.

GENTLE AROUND THE GENITALS

For reasons of hygiene, the hair growing on the penis of a male dog should be cut off at regular intervals. In the case of a bitch, the hair right around the vagina should also be removed. This being a somewhat tricky procedure, it requires the dog to stand absolutely still in order to avoid injuries.

Before bathing the dog, have the items you'll need within reach so you do not have to leave the dog unattended in the bath. First, decide where you will bathe the dog. You should have a tub or basin with a non-slip surface. Puppies can even be bathed in a sink. In warm weather, some like to use a portable pool in the yard, although you'll want to make sure your dog doesn't head for the nearest dirt pile following his bath! You will also need a hose or shower spray to wet the coat thoroughly, a shampoo formulated for dogs, absorbent towels and perhaps a blow dryer. Human shampoos are too harsh for dogs' coats and will dry them out.

Before wetting the dog, give him a brush-through to remove any dead hair, dirt and mats. Make sure he is at ease in the tub and have the water at a comfort-

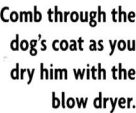

Comb through the dog's coat as you dry him with the blow dryer.

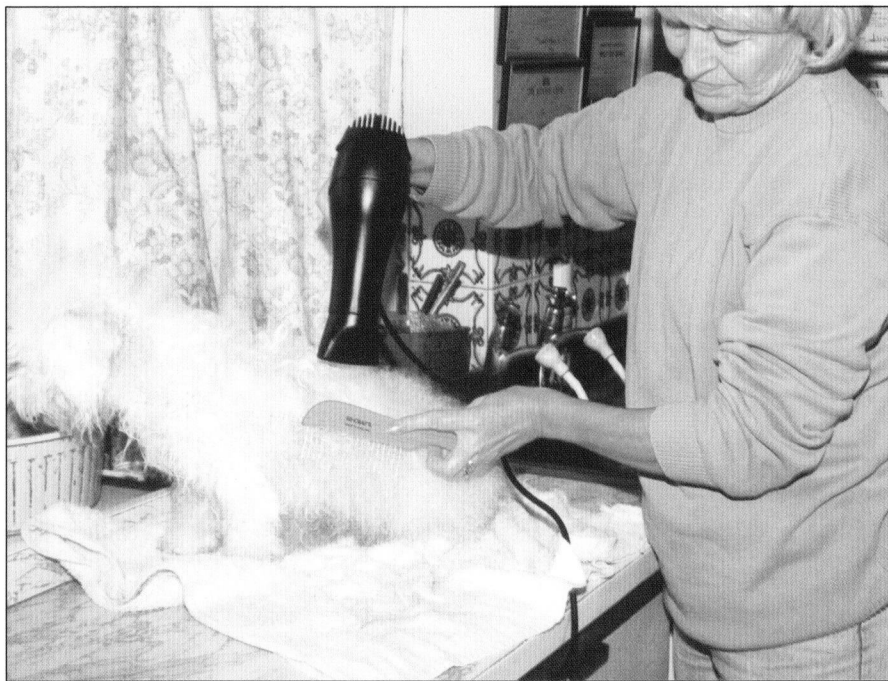

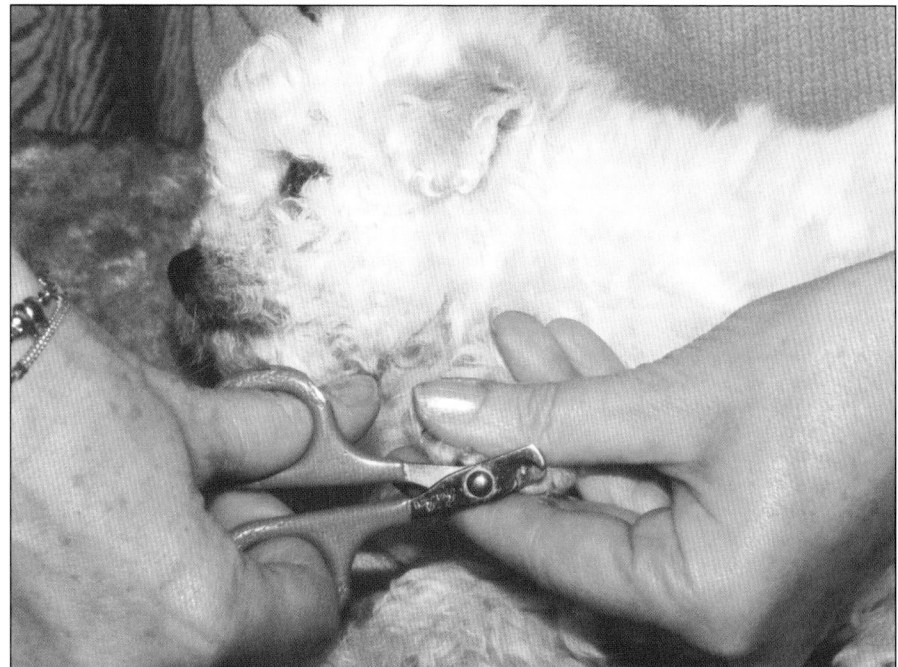

Start the nail-clipping routine with your Bolognese puppy so that he becomes accustomed to the procedure at an early age.

able temperature. Begin bathing by wetting the coat all the way down to the skin. Massage in the shampoo, keeping it away from his face and eyes. Rinse him thoroughly, again avoiding the eyes and ears, as you don't want to get water in the ear canals. A thorough rinsing is important as shampoo residue is drying and itchy to the dog. After rinsing, wrap him in a towel to absorb the initial moisture. A high-quality hair dryer with temperature control helps to prevent the hair from breaking and splitting. The dog should be dried only with lukewarm air. Once completely dry, your Bolognese should stay inside for the next three to four hours so that he doesn't get sick. It therefore may be most practical to bathe him in the evening after his last walk.

BEYOND BRUSHING
The area below the eyes must be checked daily, maybe even several times per day, for tear stains and dirt. Cleaning is most easily done with a soft cloth soaked in lukewarm water. If necessary, a tear-stain remover, available from pet shops or grooming parlors, can be applied.

In order to keep the ears clean and to prevent inflammations, you must pluck the hair

growing inside the ears at regular intervals. This aids in the unobstructed discharge of ear wax. Cleaning of the ears must never be attempted with cotton swabs, since this may actually push dirt deeper down the auditory canal. Pet shops and veterinary clinics offer a commercially made liquid ear-cleaning solution, which is applied by putting a few drops into the ear and massaging the ear so that deposits of ear wax and dirt are loosened. The outer part of the ear is then carefully wiped clean with a soft cloth. If your Bolognese carries his head at an angle all or some of the time, shakes his head frequently or tries to remove something from an ear through continual scratching, you should not hesitate to take him to a vet.

An important routine is to clean the beard of your Bolognese after every meal and comb it through carefully with a metal comb. This serves to prevent particles of his food from becoming stuck in his beard, where it may become the cause of unpleasant odors.

The length of your Bolognese's toenails should be checked on a regular basis. Since your Bolognese is "light on his feet," his nails are not worn down to a proper length through walking. As a "rule of toe," the nails should be level with the outline of the paw. They must, however, never be clipped right from the front, but rather from beneath toward the pad.

In the case of light-colored nails, it is relatively easy to determine where the "quick" (vein that runs through each nail) ends, but this is not so obvious in the case of dark-colored nails. Clipping dark nails requires a very careful approach to avoid cutting into the quick, which would be very painful to the dog and result in bleeding. Just in case, you should

Cotton swabs are not ideal for cleaning a dog's ears, as they make it too easy to probe into the ear canal, possibly causing injury and pushing debris and wax farther into the ear.

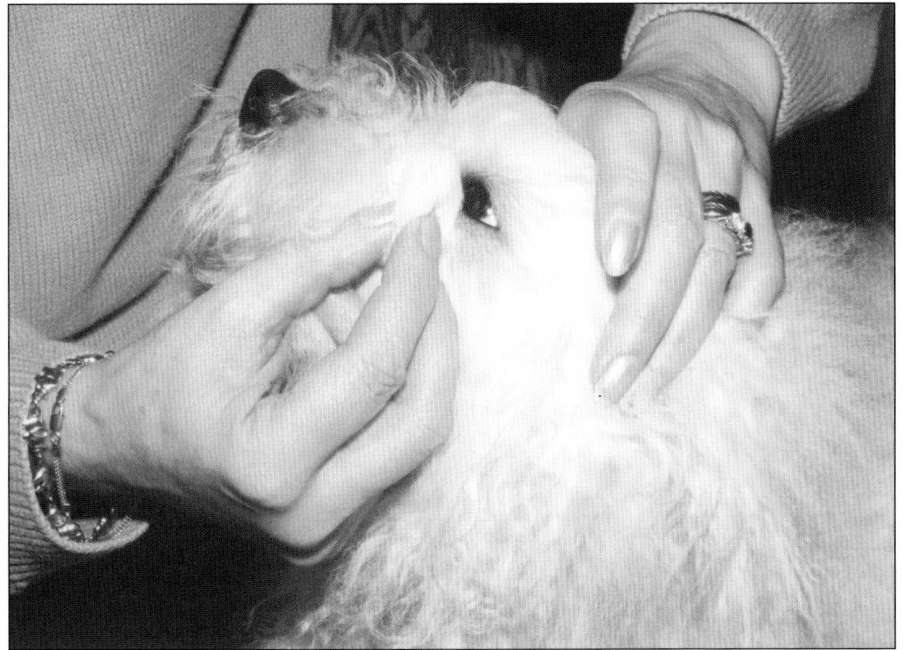

The hair around the eyes can become soiled by tear staining; clean this area gently using a damp cloth or a formula made for this purpose.

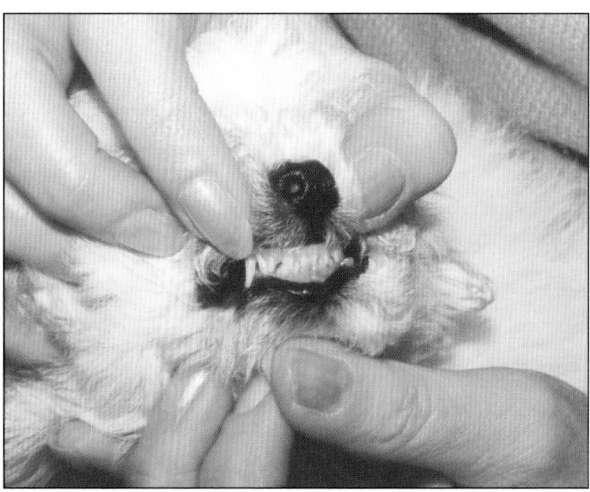

You are your dog's dentist, too. By handling a young puppy's mouth, he will learn early on to accept routine toothbrushing and mouth inspections.

have some styptic powder or chalk (the kind used for shaving) within reach to stem the flow of blood. A safer method is to use a file or electric nail grinder, at least until you learn what the proper length is. The fifth claw (dewclaw) on the forefeet must not be overlooked; if neglected, it might eventually grow inward and cut into the leg. If the dog has very brittle, hard nails, the paws may be soaked for a few minutes in lukewarm soapy water before clipping, as this makes the task substantially easier.

Some maintenance is also required in order to keep the teeth healthy. Deposits of calcium salts contained in the saliva, in conjunction with food particles and shed cells of the mucous lining of the mouth, may show as brown deposits on the bases of the teeth, commonly known as tartar. This appears to be particu-

larly common in fairly young dogs. These ugly stains are also bad-smelling. Bleeding and inflamed gums are a distinct possibility and may eventually lead to tooth loss and even problems internally as bacteria enter the bloodstream.

In order to keep your dog healthy and to ensure that he can chew his food properly, you must aim to keep his dentition complete for as long as possible (small dogs are more prone to tooth loss). Regular brushing of the teeth is important, and toothbrushes and toothpaste for dogs are readily available from pet shops. Resistant tartar can only be removed by a veterinarian, who will use ultrasonic technology. In the case of very calm dogs, this can even be done without anesthetics. Now to the other end.

You may occasionally notice your dog vigorously scooting his behind on the ground. This may be an indication of a worm infestation or a clogged anal gland. These pea-sized glands lie to the left and right of the anus in relatively large sacs and should be checked regularly, for example, during bathing.

The anal sacs should actually empty themselves during defecation. If the natural discharge is hindered, the glands have to be expressed. This is done by squeezing the sac between two fingers in an upward motion so that the accumulated mass can flow out. In some Bolognese, the procedure has to be done at regular intervals. More severe cases may require a veterinarian to perform a flushing of the anal glands. It is best to have the vet show you the proper way to express the glands before attempting it on your own; otherwise, you could injure your dog and/or end up with a smelly mess.

If you have a specific question regarding any aspect of your Bolognese's proper care, you should seek advice from your breeder, who will surely share with you his experience from years of looking after his Bolognese.

IDENTIFICATION AND TRAVEL

ID FOR YOUR DOG
You love your dog and want to keep him safe. Of course you take every precaution to prevent his escaping from the yard or becoming lost or stolen. You have a sturdy high fence and you always keep your dog on lead when out and about in public places. However, if your dog is not properly identified, you are overlooking a major aspect of his safety. We hope to never be in a situation where our dog is missing, but we should practice prevention in the unfortunate case that this happens; identification greatly increases the chances of your dog's being returned to you.

There are several ways to identify your dog. First, the traditional dog tag should be a staple in your dog's wardrobe, attached to his everyday collar. Tags can be made of sturdy plastic and various metals and should include your contact information so that a person who finds the dog can get in touch with you right away to arrange his return. Many people today enjoy the wide range of decorative tags available, so have fun and create a tag to match your dog's personality. Of course, it is important that the tag stays on the collar, so have a secure "O" ring attachment; you also can explore the type of tag that slides right onto the collar.

In addition to the ID tag, which every dog should wear even if identified by another method, two other forms of identification have become popular: microchipping and tattooing. In microchipping, a tiny scannable

Keep your Bolognese safe with proper ID and by keeping him on leash in open areas.

chip is painlessly inserted under the dog's skin. The number is registered to you so that, if your lost dog turns up at a clinic or shelter, the chip can be scanned to retrieve your contact information.

The advantage of the microchip is that it is a permanent form of ID, but there are some factors to consider. Several different companies make microchips, and not all are compatible with the others' scanning devices. It's best to find a company with a universal microchip that can be read by scanners made by other companies as well. It won't do any good to have the dog chipped if the information cannot be retrieved. Also, not every humane society, shelter and clinic is equipped with a scanner, although more and more facilities are equipping themselves. In fact, many shelters microchip dogs that

PET OR STRAY?

Besides the obvious benefit of providing your contact information to whoever finds your lost dog, an ID tag makes your dog more approachable and more likely to be recovered. A strange dog wandering the neighborhood without a collar and tags will look like a stray, while the collar and tags indicate that the dog is someone's pet. Even if the ID tags become detached from the collar, the collar alone will make a person more likely to pick up the dog.

they adopt out to new homes.

Because the microchip is not visible to the eye, the dog must wear a tag that states that he is microchipped so that whoever picks him up will know to have him scanned. The tag usually also contains the dog's microchip ID number and the registry's phone number. He of course also should have a tag with your contact information in case his chip cannot be retrieved. Humane societies and veterinary clinics offer microchipping service, which is usually very affordable.

Though less popular than microchipping, tattooing is another permanent method of ID for dogs. Most vets perform this service, and there are also clinics that perform dog tattooing. This is also an affordable procedure and one that will not cause much discomfort for the dog. It is best to put the tattoo in a visible area, such as the ear, to deter theft. It is sad to say that there are cases of dogs' being stolen and sold to research laboratories, but such laboratories will not accept tattooed dogs.

To ensure that the tattoo is effective in aiding your dog's return to you, the tattoo number must be registered with a national organization. This way, when someone finds a tattooed dog, a phone call to the registry will quickly match the dog with his owner.

HIT THE ROAD

Car travel with your dog may be limited to necessity only, such as trips to the vet, or you may bring your dog along most everywhere you go. This will depend much on your individual dog and how he reacts to rides in the car. You can begin desensitizing your Bolognese to car travel as a pup so that it's something that he's used to. Still, some dogs suffer from motion sickness. Your vet may prescribe a medication for this if trips in the car pose a problem for your dog. At the very least, you will need to get him to the vet, so he will need to tolerate these trips with the least amount of hassle possible.

Start by taking your pup on short trips, maybe just around the block. If he is fine with short trips, lengthen your rides a little at a time. Start to take him on your errands or just for drives around town. By this time it will be easy to tell if your dog is a born traveler or if he will prefer staying at home when you are on the road.

Of course, safety is a concern for dogs in the car. First, he must travel securely, not left loose to roam about the car where he could be injured or distract the driver. A young pup can be held by a passenger initially but should soon graduate to a travel crate, which can be the same crate he uses in the home. Other options include a car harness (like a seat belt for dogs) and partitioning the back of the car with a gate made for this purpose.

Bring along what you will need for the dog. He should wear his collar and ID tags, of course, and you should bring his leash, water (and food if a long trip) and clean-up materials for potty breaks and in case of motion sickness. Always keep your dog on his leash when you make stops, and never leave him alone in the car. Many a dog has died from the heat inside a closed car; this does not take much time at all. Leaving the window cracked can be dangerous if the dog tries to escape and injures himself. A dog left alone inside a car can also be a target for thieves.

UP, UP AND AWAY!

Taking a trip by air does not mean that your dog cannot accompany you, it just means that you will have to be well informed and well prepared. The majority of dogs travel as checked cargo; only the smallest of dogs are allowed in the cabin with their owners, as many airlines set a maximum crate height of 9 to 10 inches for in-cabin dogs. Your dog must travel in an airline-approved travel crate appropriate to his size so that he will be safe and comfort-able during the flight. If the crate that you use at home does not meet the airline's specifications, you can purchase one from the airline or from your pet-supply store (making sure it is labeled as airline-approved).

It's best to have the crate in advance of your trip to give the dog time to get accustomed to it. You can put a familiar blanket and a favorite toy or two in the crate with the dog to make him feel at home and to keep him occupied. The crate should be lined with absorbent material for the trip and bowls for food and water attached to the outside of the crate. The crate must be labeled with your contact information, feeding instructions (where applicable), the words "Live Animal" and arrows to indicate upright position. You will also have to provide proof of current vaccinations.

Again, advance planning is the key to smooth sailing in the skies. Make your reservations well ahead of time and know what restrictions your airline imposes: no travel during certain months, refusal of certain breeds, restrictions on certain destinations, etc. You will need to follow all of the airline's rules to help your pet enjoy a safe flight.

DOG-FRIENDLY DESTINATIONS
When planning vacations, a question that often arises is, "Who will watch the dog?" More and more families, however, are answering that question with,

"We will!" With the rise in dog-friendly places to visit, the number of families who bring their dogs along on vacation is on the rise. A search online for dog-friendly vacations will turn up many choices, as well as resources for owners of canine travelers. Ask others for suggestions: your vet, your breeder, other dog owners, breed club members, people at the local doggie daycare, etc.

Traveling with your dog means providing for his comfort and safety, and you will have to pack a bag for him just like you do for yourself (although you probably won't have liver treats in your own suitcase!). Bring his everyday items: food, water, bowls, leash and collar (with ID!), brush and comb, toys, bed, crate and any additional accessories that he will need once you get to your vacation spot. If he takes medication, don't forget to bring it with you. If going camping or on another type of outdoor excursion, take precautions to protect your dog from the sun, ticks, mosquitoes, etc. Above all, have a good time with your dog and enjoy each other's company!

BOARDING
Today there are many options for dog owners who need someone to care for their dogs in certain circumstances. While many think of boarding their dogs as

something to do when away on vacation, many others use the services of doggie "daycare" facilities, dropping their dogs off to spend the day while they are at work. Many of these facilities offer both long-term and daily care. Many go beyond just boarding and cater to all sorts of needs, with on-site grooming, veterinary care, training classes and even "web-cams" where owners can log onto the Internet and check out what their dogs are up to. Most dogs enjoy the activity and time spent with other dogs.

Before you need to use such a service, check out the ones in your area. Make visits to see the facilities, meet the staff, discuss fees and available services and see if this is a place where you think your dog will be happy. It is best to do your research in advance so that you're not stuck at the last minute, forced to make a rushed decision without knowing if the kennel that you've chosen meets your standards. You also can check with your vet's office to see if they offer boarding for their clients or if they can recommend a good kennel in the area.

The kennel will need to see proof of your dog's health records and vaccinations so as not to spread illness from dog to dog. Your dog also will need proper identification. Owners usually experience some separation anxiety the first time they have to leave their dog in someone else's care, so it's reassuring to know that the kennel you choose is run by experienced, caring, true dog people.

If possible, check to see if your breeder will board your Bolognese. This way you can trust that your dog is in good hands, and he can meet some family members too.

TRAINING YOUR

BOLOGNESE

BASIC TRAINING PRINCIPLES: PUPPY VS. ADULT

There's a big difference between training an adult dog and training a young puppy. With a young puppy, everything is new. When your pup first comes home, he will be experiencing many things, and he has nothing with which to compare these experiences. Up to this point, he has been with his dam and littermates, not one-on-one with people except in his interactions with his breeder and visitors to the litter.

When you first bring the puppy home, he is eager to please you. This means that he accepts doing things your way. During the next couple of months, he will absorb the basis of everything he needs to know for the rest of his life. This early age is even referred to as the "sponge" stage. After that, for the next 18 months, it's up to you to reinforce good manners by building on the foundation that you've established. Once your puppy is reliable in basic commands and behavior, and has reached the appropriate age, you may gradually introduce him to some of the interesting sports, games and activities available to pet owners and their dogs.

Raising your puppy is a family affair. Each member of the family must know what rules to set forth for the puppy and how to use the same one-word commands to mean exactly the same thing every time. Even if yours is a large family, one person will soon be considered by the pup to be the leader, the alpha person in his pack, the "boss" who must be obeyed. Often that highly regarded person turns out to be the one who feeds the puppy. Food ranks very high on the puppy's list of

Training is the key to molding your puppy into a good canine citizen and well-behaved family member.

important things! That's why your puppy is rewarded with small treats along with verbal praise when he responds to you correctly. As the puppy learns to do what you want him to do, the food rewards are gradually eliminated and only the praise remains. If you kept up with the food treats, you could have two problems on your hands—an obese dog and a beggar.

Training begins the minute your puppy steps through the doorway of your home, so don't make the mistake of putting the puppy on the floor and telling him by your actions, "Go for it! Run wild!" Even if this is your first puppy, you must act as if you know what you're doing: be the boss. An uncertain pup may be terrified to move, while a bold one will be ready to take you at your word and start plotting to destroy the house! Before you collected your puppy, you decided where his own special place would be, and that's where to put him when you first arrive home. Give him a house tour after he has investigated his area, had a nap and a bathroom "pit stop."

It's worth mentioning here that if you've adopted an adult dog that is completely trained to your liking, lucky you! You're off the hook! However, if that dog spent his life up to this point in a kennel, or even in a good home but without any real training, be

OUR CANINE KIDS
"Everything I learned about parenting, I learned from my dog." How often adults recognize that their parenting skills are mere extensions of the education they acquired while caring for their dogs. Many owners refer to their dogs as their "kids" and treat their canine companions like real members of the family. Surveys indicate that a majority of dog owners talk to their dogs regularly, celebrate their dogs' birthdays and purchase Christmas gifts for their dogs. Another survey shows that dog owners take their dogs to the veterinarian more frequently than they visit their own physicians.

prepared to tackle the job ahead. An adult dog with no previous training cannot be blamed for not knowing what he was never taught. While the dog is trying to understand and learn your rules, at the same time he has to unlearn many of his previously self-taught habits and general view of the world.

Working with a professional trainer will speed up your progress with an adopted adult dog. You'll need patience, too. Some new rules may be close to impossible for the dog to accept. After all, he's been successful so far by doing everything his way. (Patience again.) He may agree with your instruction for a few days and then slip back into his old ways, so you must be just as consistent and understanding in your teaching as you would be with a puppy. (More patience needed yet again.) Your dog has to learn to pay attention to your voice, your family, the daily routine, new smells, new sounds and, in some cases, even a new climate.

One of the most important things to find out about a newly adopted adult dog is his reaction to children (yours and others), strangers and your friends, and how he acts upon meeting other dogs. If he was not socialized with dogs as a puppy, this could be a major problem. This does not mean that he's a "bad" dog, a vicious dog or an aggressive dog; rather, it means that he has no idea how to read another dog's body language. There's no way for him to tell if the other dog is a friend or foe. Survival instinct takes over, telling him to attack first and ask questions later. This definitely calls for professional help and, even then, may not be a behavior that can be corrected 100% reliably (or even at all). If you have a puppy, this is why it is so very important to introduce your young puppy properly to other puppies and "dog-friendly" adult dogs.

HOUSE-TRAINING

Dogs are tactility-oriented when it comes to house-training. In other words, they respond to the surface on which they are given approval to eliminate. The choice is yours (the dog's version is in parentheses): The lawn (including the neighbors' lawns)? A bare patch of earth under a tree (where people like to sit and relax in the summertime)? Concrete steps or patio (all sidewalks, garages and basement floors)? The curbside (watch out for cars)? A small area of crushed stone in a corner of the yard (mine!)? The latter is the best choice if you can manage it, because it will remain strictly for the dog's use and is easy to keep clean.

You can start out with paper-training indoors and switch over to an outdoor surface as the puppy matures and gains control over his need to eliminate. For the naysayers, don't worry—this won't mean that the dog will soil on every piece of newspaper lying around the house. You are training him to go outside, remember? Starting out by paper-training often is the only choice for a city dog.

WHEN YOUR PUPPY'S "GOT TO GO"
Your puppy's need to relieve himself is seemingly non-stop, but signs of improvement will be seen each week. For about the first 2 weeks, the puppy will have to be taken outside every time he wakes up, about 10–15 minutes after every meal and after every period

of play—all day long, from first thing in the morning until his bedtime. That's a total of ten or more trips per day to teach the puppy where it's okay to relieve himself. With that schedule in mind, you can see that house-training a young puppy is not a part-time job. It requires someone to be home all day.

If that seems overwhelming or impossible, do a little planning. For example, plan to pick up your puppy at the start of a vacation period. If you can't get home in the middle of the day, plan to hire a dog-sitter or ask a neighbor to come over to take the pup outside, feed him his lunch and then take him out again about ten or so minutes after he's eaten. Also make arrangements with that or another person to be your "emergency" contact if you have to stay late on the job. Remind yourself—repeatedly—that this hectic schedule improves as the puppy gets older.

HOME WITHIN A HOME

Your puppy needs to be confined to one secure, puppy-proof area when no one is able to watch his every move. Generally, the kitchen is the place of choice because the floor is washable. Likewise, it's a busy family area that will accustom the pup to a variety of noises, everything from pots and pans to the telephone, blender and dishwasher. He will also be enchanted by the smell of your cooking (and will never be critical when you burn something). An exercise pen (also called an "ex-pen," a puppy version of a playpen) within the room of choice is an excellent means of confinement for a young pup. He can see out and has a certain amount of space in which to run about, but he is safe from dangerous things like electrical cords, heating units, trash baskets or open kitchen-supply cabinets. Place the pen where the puppy will not get a blast of heat or air conditioning, and make sure that the pen is sturdy with high sides so the pup cannot climb out.

Your Bolognese can't tell you when it's time to go, but his actions will. Look for these signals in order to properly house-train your pup.

You can start toilet training indoors using newspaper.

In the pen, you can put a few toys, his bed (which can be his crate if the dimensions of pen and crate are compatible) and a few layers of newspaper in one small corner, just in case. A water bowl can be hung at a convenient height on the side of the ex-pen so it won't become a splashing pool for an innovative puppy. His food dish can go on the floor, next to but not under the water bowl.

Crates are something that pet owners are at last getting used to for their dogs. Wild or domestic canines have always preferred to sleep in den-like safe spots, and that is exactly what the crate provides. How often have you seen adult dogs that choose to sleep under a table or chair even though they have full run of the house? It's the den connection.

The crate can be solid (fiberglass) with ventilation on the upper sides and a wire-grate door that locks securely or it can be of open wire construction with a solid floor, also with a locking door. Your puppy will go along with whichever one you prefer. The open wire crate, however, should be covered at night to give the snug feeling of a den. A blanket or towel over the top will be fine.

The crate should be big enough for the adult dog to stand up and turn around in, even though he may spend much of his time curled up in the back part of it. Never afford a young puppy too much space, thinking that you're being kind and generous. He'll just sleep at one end of the crate and soil in the other end! While you should purchase only one crate, one that will accommodate your pup when grown, you may need to make use of a removable crate partition so that the pup has a comfortable area without enough extra space to use as a toilet. A dog does not like to soil where he sleeps, so you are teaching him to "hold it" until it's time for a trip outside. You may want an extra crate to keep in the car for safe traveling.

In your "happy" voice, use the word "Crate" every time you put the pup in his den. If he's new to a crate, toss in a small biscuit for him to chase the first few times. At night, after he's been outside, he should sleep in his crate. The crate may be kept in his designated area at night or, if you want to be sure to hear those wake-up yips in the morning, put the crate in a corner of your bedroom. However, don't make any response whatsoever to whining or crying. If he's completely ignored, he'll settle down and get to sleep.

Good bedding for a young puppy is an old folded bath towel or an old blanket, something that is easily washable and disposable if necessary ("accidents" will happen!). Never put newspaper in the puppy's crate. Those old ideas of adding a clock to replace his mother's heartbeat, or a hot-water bottle to replace her warmth, are just that—old ideas. The clock could drive the puppy nuts, and the hot-water bottle could end up

With diligence on your part, your puppy will soon be letting you know when it's time to go out—don't ignore him!

Some breeders introduce the pups to crates for short periods of time, giving owners an advantage in crate-training.

family as long as there is someone responsible for watching him. That doesn't mean just someone in the same room who is watching TV or busy on the computer, but one person who is doing nothing other than keeping an eye on the pup, playing with him on the floor and helping him understand his position in the pack.

This first taste of freedom will let you begin to set the house rules. If you don't want the dog on the furniture, now is the time to prevent his first attempts to jump up on the couch. The word to use in this case is "Off," not "Down." "Down" is the word you will use to teach the down position, which is something entirely different.

Most corrections at this stage come in the form of simply distracting the puppy. Instead of telling him "No" for "Don't chew the carpet," distract the chomping puppy with a toy and he'll forget about the carpet.

As you are playing with the pup, do not forget to watch him closely and pay attention to his body language. Whenever you see him begin to circle or sniff, take the puppy outside to relieve himself. If you are paper-training, put him back in his confined area on the newspapers. In either case, praise him as he eliminates, while he actually is *in the act* of relieving himself. Three seconds after he has finished is too late!

as a very soggy waterbed! An extremely good breeder would have introduced your puppy to the crate by letting two pups sleep together for a couple of nights, followed by several nights alone. How thankful you will be if you found that breeder!

Safe toys in the pup's crate or area will keep him occupied, but monitor their condition closely. Discard any toys that show signs of being chewed to bits. Squeaky parts, bits of stuffing or plastic or any other small pieces can cause intestinal blockage or possibly choking if swallowed.

PROGRESSING WITH POTTY-TRAINING
After you've taken your puppy out and he has relieved himself in the area you've selected, he can have some free time with the

You'll be praising him for running toward you, picking up a toy or whatever he may be doing at that moment, and that's not what you want to be praising him for. Timing is a vital tool in all dog training. Use it.

Remove soiled newspapers immediately and replace them with clean ones. You may want to take a small piece of soiled paper and place it in the middle of the new clean papers, as the scent will attract him to that spot when it's time to go again. That scent attraction is why it's so important to clean up any messes made in the house with a product specially made to eliminate the odor of dog urine and droppings. Regular household cleansers won't do the trick. Pet shops sell the best pet deodorizers. Invest in the largest container you can find.

Scent attraction eventually will lead your pup to his chosen spot outdoors, too; this is the basis of outdoor training. When you take your puppy outside to relieve himself, use a one-word command such as "Outside" or "Go-potty" (that's one word to the puppy!) as you pick him up and attach his leash. Then put him down in his area. If for some reason you cannot carry him, snap the leash on quickly and lead him to his spot. Now comes the hard part—hard for you, that is. Just stand there until he urinates and defecates. Move him a few feet in one direction or another if he's just sitting there, looking at you, but remember that this is neither playtime nor time for a walk. This is strictly a business trip. Then, as he circles and squats (remember your timing!), give him a quiet "Good dog" as praise. If you start to jump for joy, ecstatic over his performance, he'll do one of two things: either he will stop mid-

SOMEBODY TO BLAME

House-training a puppy can be frustrating for the puppy and the owner alike. The puppy does not instinctively understand the difference between defecating on the pavement outside and on the ceramic tile in the kitchen. He is confused and frightened by his human's exuberant reactions to his natural urges. The owner, arguably the more intelligent of the duo, is also frustrated that he cannot convince his puppy to obey his commands and instructions.

In frustration, the owner may struggle with the temptation to discipline the puppy, scold him or even strike him on the rear end. Harsh corrections are unnecessary and inappropriate, serving to defeat your purpose in gaining your puppy's trust and respect. Don't blame your nine-week-old puppy. Blame yourself for not being 100% consistent in the puppy's lessons and routine. The lesson here is simple: try harder and your puppy will succeed.

stream, as it were, or he'll do it again for you—in the house—and expect you to be just as delighted!

Give him five minutes or so and, if he doesn't go in that time, take him back indoors to his confined area and try again in another ten minutes, or immediately if you see him sniffing and circling. By careful observation, you'll soon work out a successful schedule.

Accidents, by the way, are just that—accidents. Clean them up quickly and thoroughly, without comment, after the puppy has been taken outside to finish his business and then put back in his area or crate. If you witness an accident in progress, say "No!" in a stern voice and get the pup outdoors immediately. No punishment is needed. You and your puppy are just learning each other's language and sometimes it's easy to miss a puppy's message. Chalk it up to experience and watch more closely from now on.

KEEPING THE PACK ORDERLY
Discipline is a form of training that brings order to life. For example, military discipline is what allows the soldiers in an army to work as one. Discipline is a form of teaching and, in dogs, is the basis of how the successful pack operates. Each member knows his place in the

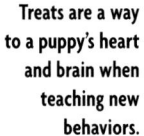

Treats are a way to a puppy's heart and brain when teaching new behaviors.

pack and all respect the leader, or alpha dog. It is essential for your puppy that you establish this type of relationship, with you as the alpha, or leader. It is a form of social coexistence that all canines recognize and accept. Discipline, therefore, is never to be confused with punishment. When you teach your puppy how you want him to behave, and he behaves properly and you praise him for it, you are disciplining him with a form of positive reinforcement.

For a dog, rewards come in the form of praise, a smile, a cheerful tone of voice, a few friendly pats or a rub of the ears. Rewards are also small food treats. Obviously, that does not mean bits of regular dog food. Rather, treats are very small bits of special things like cheese or pieces of soft dog treats. The idea is to reward the dog with something very small that he can taste and swallow, providing instant positive reinforcement. If he has to take time to chew the treat, by the time he is finished, he will have forgotten what he did to earn it!

Your puppy should never be physically punished. The displeasure shown on your face and in your voice is sufficient to signal to the pup that he has done something wrong. He wants to please everyone higher up on the social ladder, especially his

leader, so a scowl and harsh voice will take care of the error. Growling out the word "Shame!" when the pup is caught in the act of doing something wrong is better than the repetitive "No." Some dogs hear "No" so often that they begin to think it's their name! By the way, do not use the dog's name when you're correcting him. His name is reserved to get his attention for something pleasant about to take place.

There are punishments that have nothing to do with you. For example, your dog may think that chasing cats is one reason for his existence. You can try to stop it as much as you like without success because it's such fun for the dog. But one good hissing, spitting swipe of a cat's claws across the dog's nose will put an end to the game forever. Only intervene when your dog's

SHOULD WE ENROLL?

If you have the means and the time, you should definitely take your dog to obedience classes. Begin with puppy kindergarten classes in which puppies of all sizes learn basic lessons while getting the opportunity to meet and greet each other; it's as much about socialization as it is about good manners. What you learn in class you can practice at home. And if you goof up in practice, you'll get help in the next session.

eyeball is seriously at risk. Cat scratches can cause permanent damage to an innocent but annoying puppy.

PUPPY KINDERGARTEN

COLLAR AND LEASH

Before you begin your puppy's education, he must be used to his collar and leash. Choose a collar for your puppy that is secure but not heavy or bulky. He won't enjoy training if he's uncomfortable. A flat buckle collar is fine for everyday wear and for initial puppy training. Do not use a chain choke collar with your Bolognese. Not only is the chain choke collar unsuitable for small dogs like the Bolognese but it will also pull at and damage the breed's long coat.

A lightweight 6-foot woven cotton or nylon training leash is preferred by most trainers because it is easy to fold up in your hand and comfortable to hold because there is a certain amount of give to it. There are lessons where the dog will start off 6 feet away from you at the end of the leash. The leash used to take the puppy outside to relieve himself is shorter because you don't want him to roam away from his area. The shorter leash will also be the one to use when you walk the puppy for the same reason.

If you've been wise enough to enroll in a puppy kindergarten class, suggestions will be made as to the best collar and leash for your young puppy. I say "wise" because your puppy will be in a class with puppies in his age range (up to five months old) of all breeds and sizes. It's the perfect way for him to learn the right way (and the wrong way) to interact with other dogs as well as their people. You cannot teach your puppy how to interpret another dog's sign language. For a first-time puppy owner, these socialization classes are invaluable. For experienced dog owners, they are a real boon to further training.

ATTENTION

You've been using the dog's name since the minute you collected him from the breeder, so you should be able to get his attention by saying his name—with a big smile and in an excited tone of

---

A SMILE'S WORTH A MILE

Don't embark on your puppy's training course when you're not in the mood. Never train your puppy if you're feeling grouchy or impatient with him. Subjecting your puppy to your bad mood is a bad move. Your pup will sense your negative attitude, and neither of you will enjoy the session or have any measure of success. Always begin and end your training sessions on a happy note.

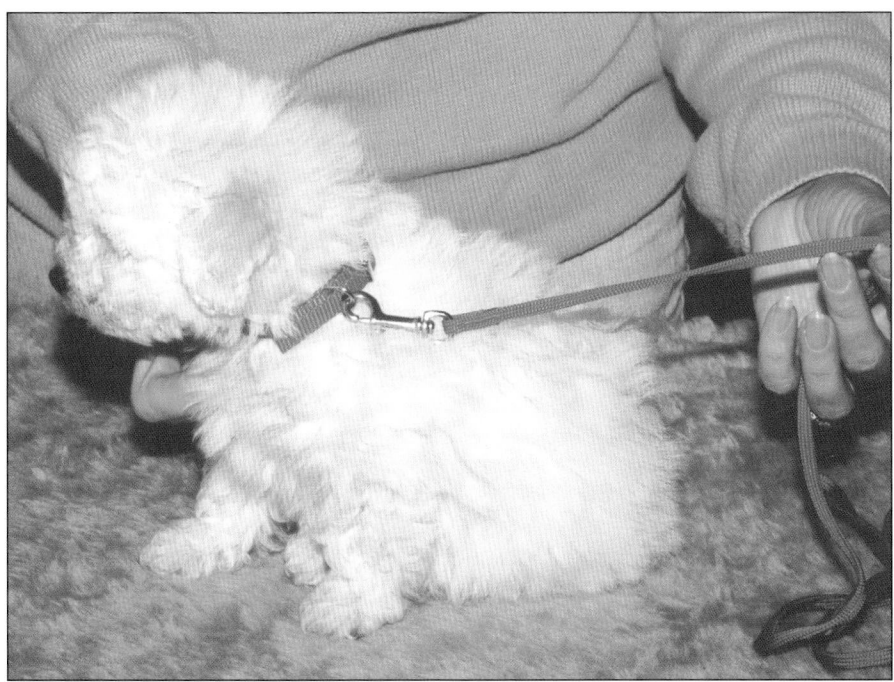

voice. His response will be the puppy equivalent of "Here I am! What are we going to do?" Your immediate response (if you haven't guessed by now) is "Good dog." Rewarding him at the moment he pays attention to you teaches him the proper way to respond when he hears his name.

EXERCISES FOR A BASIC CANINE EDUCATION

THE SIT EXERCISE
Sit is usually one of the first commands taught, as it is learned quickly and forms the basis of other exercises. There are several ways to teach the puppy to sit.

The first one is to catch him whenever he is about to sit and, as his backside nears the floor, say "Sit, good dog!" That's positive reinforcement and, if your timing is sharp, he will learn that what he's doing at that second is connected to your saying "Sit" and that you think he's clever for doing it!

Another method is to start with the puppy on his leash in front of you. Show him a treat in the palm of your right hand. Bring your hand up under his nose and, almost in slow motion, move your hand up and back so his nose goes up in the air and his head tilts back as he follows the treat in your hand. At that point, he will have to either sit or fall over, so as his back legs buckle under, say "Sit, good dog," and then give him the treat and lots of praise. You may have to begin with your hand lightly running up his chest, actually lifting his chin up until he sits. Some (usually older) dogs require gentle pressure on their hindquarters with the left hand, in which case the dog should be on your left side. Puppies generally do not appreciate this physical dominance.

After a few times, you should be able to show the dog a treat in the open palm of your hand, raise your hand waist-high as you say "Sit" and have him sit. You thereby will have taught him two things at the same time. The verbal command and the motion of the hand are both signals for

READY, SIT, GO!

On your marks, get set: train! Most professional trainers agree that the sit command is the place to start your dog's formal education. Sitting is a natural posture for most dogs, and they respond to the sit exercise willingly and readily. For every lesson, begin with the sit command so that you start out on a successful note; likewise, you should practice the sit command at the end of every lesson as well, because you always want to end on a high note.

the sit. Your puppy is watching you almost more than he is listening to you, so what you do is just as important as what you say.

Don't save any of these drills only for training sessions. Use them as much as possible at odd times during a normal day. The dog should always sit before being given his food dish. He should sit to let you go through a doorway first, when the doorbell rings or when you stop to speak to someone on the street.

THE DOWN EXERCISE

Before beginning to teach the down command, you must consider how the dog feels about this exercise. To him, "Down" is a submissive position. Being flat on the floor with you standing over him is not his idea of fun. It's up to you to let him know that, while it may not be fun, the reward of your approval is worth his effort.

Start with the puppy on your left side in a sit position. Hold the leash right above his collar in your left hand. Have an extra-special treat, such as a small piece of cooked chicken or hot dog, in your right hand. Place it at the end of the pup's nose and steadily move your hand down and forward along the ground. Hold the leash to prevent a sudden lunge for the food. As the puppy goes into the down position, say "Down" very gently.

The difficulty with this exercise is twofold: It's both the submissive aspect and the fact that most people say the word "Down" as if they were drill sergeants in charge of recruits! So issue the command sweetly, give him the treat and have the pup maintain the down position for several seconds. If he tries to get up immediately, place your hands on his shoulders and press down gently, giving him a very quiet "Good dog." As you progress with this lesson, increase the "down time" until he will hold it until you say "Okay" (his cue for release). Practice this one in the house at various times throughout the day.

By increasing the length of time during which the dog must maintain the down position, you'll find many uses for it. For example, he can lie at your feet in the vet's office or anywhere that both of you have to wait, when you are on the phone, while the family is eating and so forth. If you progress to training for competitive obedience, he'll already be all set for the exercise called the "long down."

THE STAY EXERCISE

To teach the sit/stay, have the dog sit on your left side. Hold the leash at waist level in your left hand and let the dog know that you have a treat in your closed right hand. Step forward on your

right foot as you say "Stay." Immediately turn and stand directly in front of the dog, keeping your right hand up high so he'll keep his eye on the treat hand and maintain the sit position for a count of five. Return to your original position and offer the reward.

Increase the length of the sit/stay each time until the dog can hold it for at least 30 seconds without moving. After about a week of success, move out on your right foot and take two steps before turning to face the dog. Give the "Stay" hand signal (left palm held up, facing the dog) as you leave. He gets the treat when you return and he holds the sit/stay. Increase the distance that you walk away from him before turning until you reach the length of your training leash. But don't

"Down" is a natural position for most dogs, except when commanded to do so.

Greet your puppy with positive attention every time he comes to you to encourage him to come when called.

rush it. Go back to the beginning if he moves before he should. No matter what the lesson, never be upset by having to back up for a few days. The repetition and practice are what will make your dog reliable in these commands. It won't do any good to move on to something more difficult if the command is not mastered at the easier levels. Above all, even if you do get frustrated, never let your puppy know. Always keep a positive, upbeat attitude during training, which will transmit to your dog for positive results.

The down/stay is taught in the same way once the dog is completely reliable and steady with the down command. Again, don't rush it. With the dog in the down position on your left side, step out on your right foot as you say "Stay." Return by walking around in back of the dog and into your original position. While you are training, it's okay to murmur something like "Hold on" to encourage him to stay put. When the dog will stay without moving when you are at a distance of 3 or 4 feet, begin to increase the length of time before you return. Be sure he holds the down on your return until you say "Okay." At that point, he gets his treat—just so he'll remember for next time that it's not over until it's over.

THE COME EXERCISE

No command is more important to the safety of your dog than "Come." It is what you should say every single time you see the puppy running toward you: "Romeo, come! Good dog." During playtime, run a few feet away from the puppy, turn and tell him to "Come" as he is already running to you. You can go so far as to teach your puppy two things at once if you squat down and hold out your arms. As the pup gets close to you and you're saying "Good dog," bring your right arm in about waist-high. Now he's also learning the hand signal, an excellent device should you be on the phone when you need to get him to come to you. You'll also both be one step ahead when you enter obedience classes.

When the puppy responds to your well-timed "Come," try it with the puppy on the training leash. This time, catch him off guard, while he's sniffing a leaf or watching a bird: "Romeo, come!" You may have to pause for a split second after his name to be sure you have his attention. If the

puppy shows any sign of confusion, give the leash a mild jerk and take a couple of steps backward. Do not repeat the command. In this case, as he reaches you, you should say "Good come!"

An important rule of training is that each command word is given just once. Anything more is nagging. You'll also notice that all commands are one word only. Even when they are actually two words, you say them as one.

Never call the dog to come to you—with or without his name— if you are angry or intend to correct him for some misbehavior. When correcting the pup, you go to him. Your dog must always connect "Come" with something pleasant and with your approval; then you can rely on his response. Puppies, like children, have notoriously short attention spans, so don't overdo it with any of the

OKAY!
This is the signal that tells your dog that he can quit whatever he was doing. Use "Okay" to end a session on a correct response to a command. (Never end on an incorrect response.) Lots of praise follows. People use "Okay" a lot and it has other uses for dogs, too. Your dog is barking. You say, "Okay! Come!" "Okay" signals him to stop the barking activity and "Come" allows him to come to you for a "Good dog."

TIPS FOR
TRAINING AND SAFETY

1. Whether on or off leash, practice only in a fenced area.
2. Remove the training collar when the training session is over.
3. Don't try to break up a dogfight.
4. "Come," "Leave it" and "Wait" are safety commands.
5. The dog belongs in a crate or behind a barrier when riding in the car.
6. Don't ignore the dog's first sign of aggression. Aggression only gets worse, so take it seriously.
7. Keep the faces of children and dogs separated.
8. Pay attention to what the dog is chewing.
9. Keep the vet's number near your phone.
10. "Okay" is a useful release command.

training. Keep each lesson short. Break it up with a quick run around the yard or a ball toss, repeat the lesson and quit as soon as the pup gets it right. That way, you will always end with a "Good dog." Life isn't perfect and neither are puppies. A time will come, often around ten months of age, when he'll become "selectively deaf" or choose to "forget" his name. He may respond by wagging his tail (and even seeming to smile at you) with a look that says "Make me!" Laugh, throw his favorite toy and skip the lesson you had planned. Pups will be pups!

THE HEEL EXERCISE

The second most important command to teach, after the come, is the heel. When you are walking your growing puppy, you need to be in control. Besides, it's no fun to walk a dog who pulls ahead, lags behind or generally acts crazy on the leash. Your young puppy will probably follow you everywhere, but that's his natural instinct, not your control over the situation. However, any time he does follow you, you can say "Heel" and be ahead of the game, as he will learn to associate this command with the action of following you before you even begin teaching him to heel.

There is a very precise, almost military, procedure for teaching your dog to heel. As with all obedience training, begin with the dog on your left side. He will be sitting nicely and you will have the training leash across your chest. Hold the loop and folded leash in your right hand. Pick up the slack leash above the dog in your left hand and hold it loosely at your side. Step out on your left foot as you say "Heel." If the puppy does not move, give a gentle tug or pat your left leg to get him started. If he surges ahead of you, stop and pull him back gently until he is at your side. Tell him to sit and begin again.

Walk a few steps and stop while the puppy is correctly beside you. Tell him to sit and give mild verbal praise. (More enthusiastic praise will encourage him to think the lesson is over.) Repeat the lesson, only increasing the number of steps you take as long as the dog is heeling nicely beside you. When you end the lesson, have him hold the sit, then give him the "Okay" to let him know that this is the end of the lesson. Praise him so that he knows he did a good job.

The cure for excessive pulling (a common problem) is to stop when the dog is no more than 2 or 3 feet ahead of you. Guide him back into position and begin again. With a really determined puller, try switching to a head collar. When used properly, this will automatically turn the pup's head toward you so you can bring him back easily to the heel position. Give quiet, reassuring praise every time the leash goes slack and he's staying with you.

Heeling lessons can take a lot out of a dog, so provide playtime and free-running exercise when the lessons are over to shake off the stress. You don't want him to associate training with all work and no fun.

TAPERING OFF TIDBITS
Your dog has been watching you—and the hand that treats—throughout all of his lessons, and now it's time to break the treat habit. Begin by giving him treats at the end of each lesson only. Then start to give a treat after the end of only some of the lessons. At the end of every lesson, as well as during the lessons, be consistent with the praise. Your pup now doesn't know if he'll get a treat or not, but he should keep performing well just in case! Finally, you will stop giving treat rewards entirely. Save them for something brand-new that you want to teach him. Keep up the praise and you'll always have a "good dog."

OBEDIENCE CLASSES
The advantages of an obedience class are that your dog will have to learn amid the distractions of other people and dogs and that your mistakes will be quickly

Not only will obedience classes teach your Bolognese proper behaviors he will also learn how to behave properly around other canines.

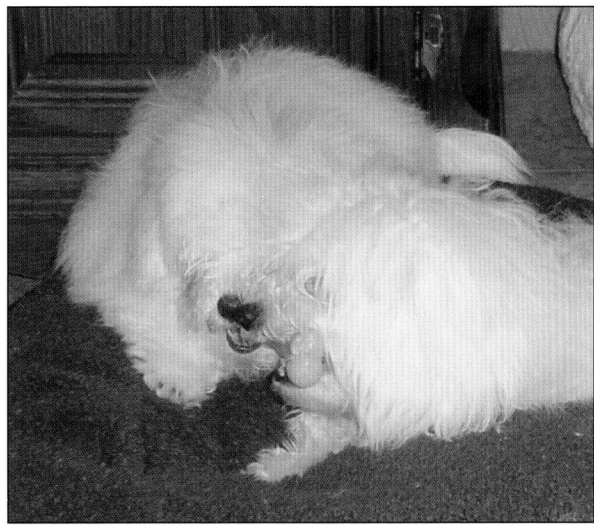

All dogs are individuals and training will be different from one dog to the next. For the most part though, Bolognese are quite trainable.

corrected by the trainer. Teaching your dog along with a qualified instructor and other handlers who may have more dog experience than you are further benefits of the class environment. The instructor and other handlers can help you to find the most efficient way of teaching your dog a command or exercise, so not only will your dog be learning but you also will be learning how to teach your dog. It's often easier to learn by other people's mistakes than your own. You will also learn all of the requirements for competitive obedience trials, in which your dog can earn titles and go on to advanced jumping and retrieving exercises, which are fun for many dogs. Obedience classes build the

foundation needed for many other canine activities (in which we humans are allowed to participate, too!).

TRAINING YOUR BOLOGNESE FOR OTHER ACTIVITIES

Once your dog has basic obedience under his collar, and is 12 months of age, you can enter the world of agility training. Dogs think agility is pure fun, like being turned loose in an amusement park full of obstacles! Agility is fun for owners, too, as owners run through the agility course with their dogs to guide them through the exercises in proper order. For those who like to volunteer, there is the wonderful feeling of owning a therapy dog and visiting hospices, nursing homes and veterans' homes to bring smiles, comfort and companionship to those who live there, and the friendly, affectionate Bolognese is certainly a welcome sight.

Around the house, your Bolognese can be taught to do some simple chores. You might teach him to carry or fetch small household items. The kids can teach the dog all kinds of tricks, from playing hide-and-seek to balancing a biscuit on his nose. A family dog is what rounds out the family. Everything he does, including sitting in your lap or gazing lovingly at you, represents the bonus of owning a dog.

Showing is a popular activity for Bolognese and their owners. The Bolognese is a beautiful sight in the show ring and is seen often at rare-breed events. Bolognese destined for the show ring should receive early training in the special disciplines required of conformation show dogs.

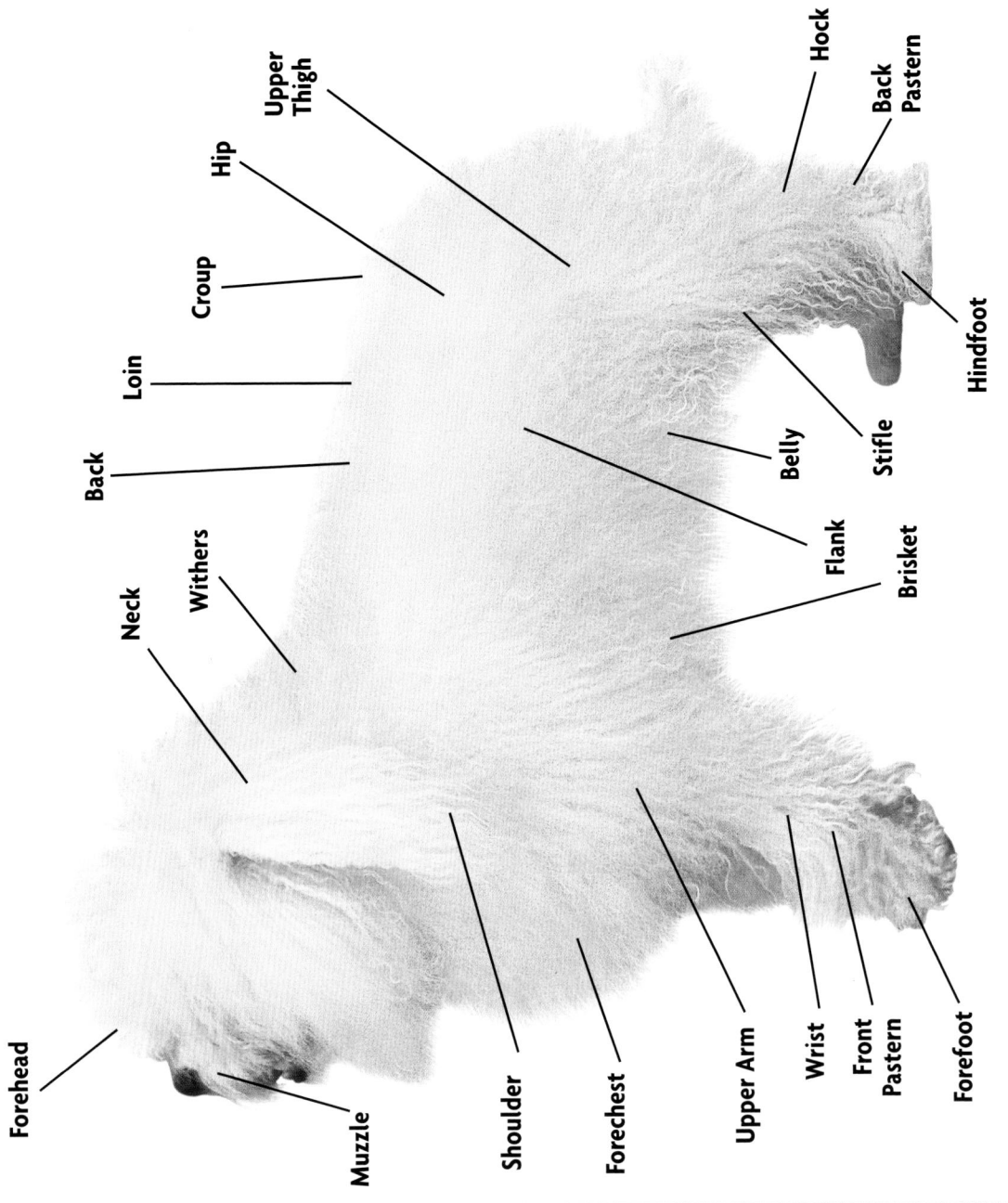

Hock

Back
Pastern

Upper
Thigh

Hip

Hindfoot

Croup

Loin

Belly

Stifle

Back

Flank

Withers

Brisket

Neck

Forehead

Muzzle

Shoulder

Forechest

Upper Arm

Wrist

Front
Pastern

Forefoot

PHYSICAL STRUCTURE OF THE BOLOGNESE

HEALTHCARE OF YOUR

BOLOGNESE

By Lowell Ackerman DVM, DACVD

HEALTHCARE FOR A LIFETIME
When you own a dog, you become his healthcare advocate over his entire lifespan, as well as being the one to shoulder the financial burden of such care. Accordingly, it is worthwhile to focus on prevention rather than treatment, as you and your pet will both be happier.

Of course, the best place to have begun your program of preventive healthcare is with the initial purchase or adoption of your dog. There is no way of guaranteeing that your new furry friend is free of medical problems, but there are some things you can do to improve your odds. You certainly should have done adequate research into the Bolognese and have selected your puppy carefully rather than buying on impulse. Health issues aside, a large number of pet abandonment and relinquishment cases arise from a mismatch between pet needs and owner expectations. This is entirely preventable with appropriate planning and finding a good breeder.

Regarding healthcare issues specifically, it is very difficult to make blanket statements about where to acquire a problem-free pet, but, again, a reputable breeder is your best bet. In an ideal situation, you have the opportunity to see both parents, get references from other owners of the breeder's pups and see genetic-testing documentation for several generations of the litter's ancestors. At the very least, you must thoroughly investigate the Bolognese and the problems inherent in the breed, as well as the genetic testing available to screen for those problems. Genetic testing offers some important benefits but is only available for a few disorders in a relatively small number of breeds and is not available for some of the most common genetic diseases, such as patellar luxation, cataracts, epilepsy, cardiomyopathy, etc. This area of research is indeed exciting and increasingly important, and advances will continue to be made each year. In fact, recent research has shown that there is an equivalent dog gene for 75% of known human genes, so research done in either species is likely to benefit the other.

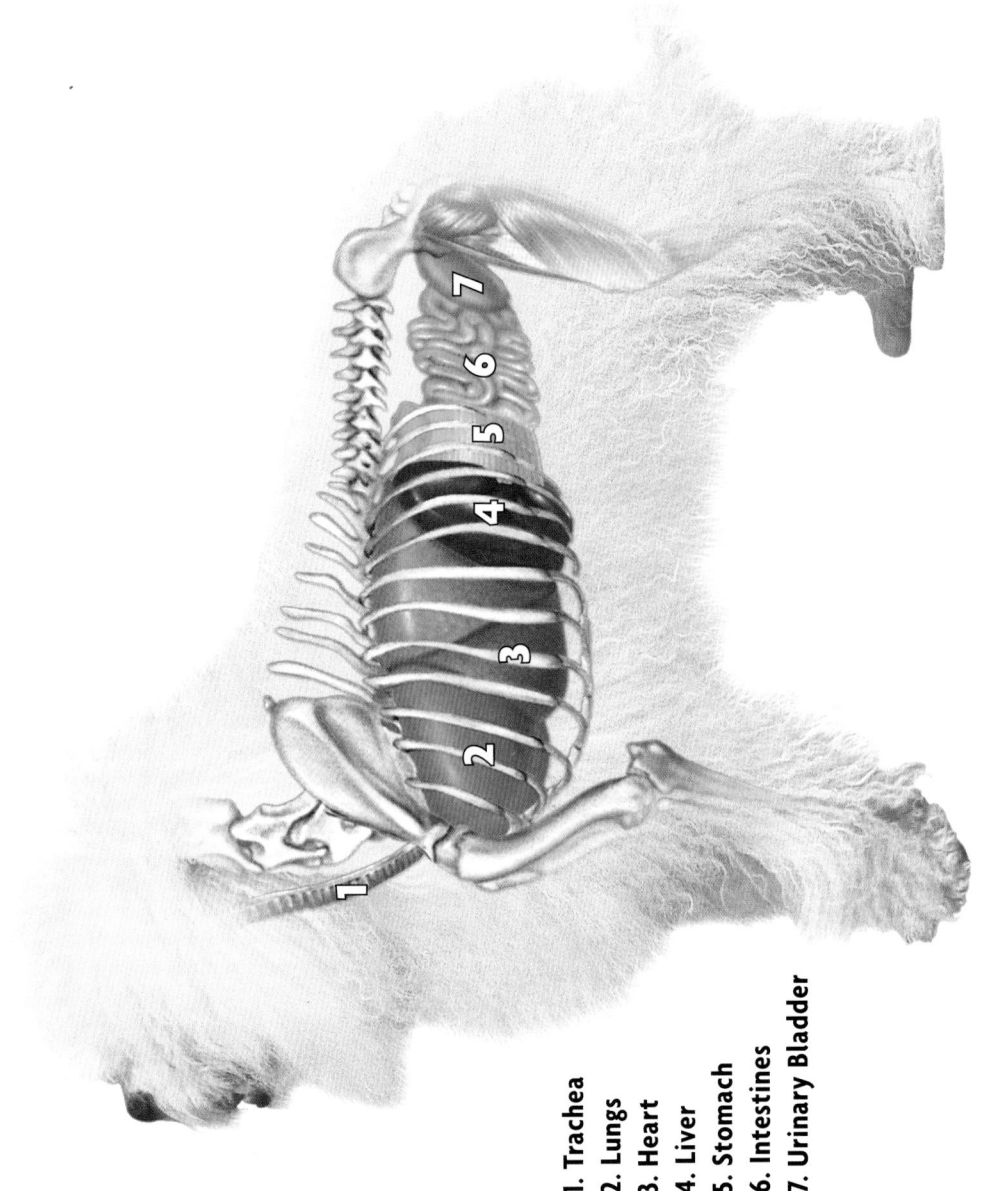

1. Trachea
2. Lungs
3. Heart
4. Liver
5. Stomach
6. Intestines
7. Urinary Bladder

INTERNAL ORGANS OF THE BOLOGNESE

We've also discussed that evaluating your chosen pup's behavioral nature and that of his immediate family members is an important part of the selection process that cannot be underestimated or overemphasized. It is sometimes difficult to evaluate temperament in puppies because certain behavioral tendencies, such as some forms of aggression, may not be immediately evident. More dogs are euthanized each year for behavioral reasons than for all medical conditions combined, so it is critical to take temperament issues seriously. Start with a well-balanced, friendly companion and put the time and effort into proper socialization, and you will both be rewarded with a valued relationship for the dog's lifetime.

With a pup from healthy, sound stock, you become responsible for helping your veterinarian keep your pet healthy. Some crucial things happen before you even bring your puppy home. Parasite control typically begins at two weeks of age and vaccinations typically begin at six to eight weeks of age. A pre-pubertal evaluation is typically scheduled for about six months of age. At this time, a dental evaluation is done (since the adult teeth are now in), heartworm prevention is started and neutering or spaying is most commonly done.

Most dogs are considered adults at a year of age, although some larger breeds still have some filling out to do up to about two or so years old. Each breed has different healthcare requirements, so work with your veterinarian to determine what will be needed and what your role should be. This doctor-client relationship is important, because as vaccination guidelines change, there may not be an annual "vaccine visit" scheduled. You must make sure that you see your veterinarian at least annually, even if no vaccines are due, because this is the best opportunity to coordinate healthcare activities and to make sure that no medical issues creep by unaddressed.

When your pet reaches three-quarters of his anticipated lifespan, he is considered a "senior" and likely requires some special care. In general, if you've

With the proper healthcare, these ten-day-old Bolognese will have a long and happy life ahead of them.

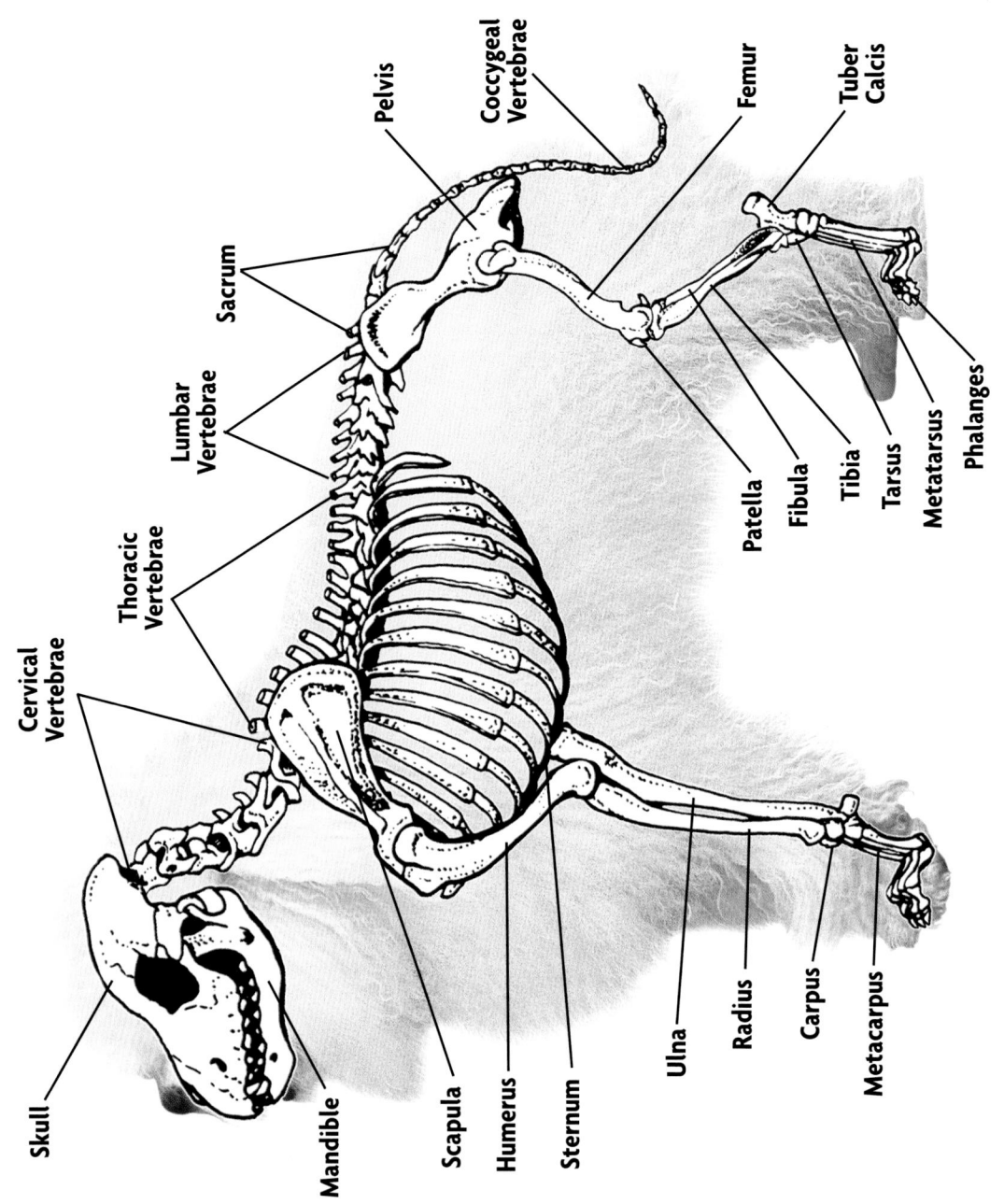

Coccygeal Vertebrae

Femur

Tuber Calcis

Pelvis

Sacrum

Lumbar Vertebrae

Thoracic Vertebrae

Patella

Fibula

Tibia

Tarsus

Metatarsus

Phalanges

Cervical Vertebrae

Skull

Mandible

Scapula

Humerus

Sternum

Ulna

Radius

Carpus

Metacarpus

SKELETAL STRUCTURE OF THE BOLOGNESE

been taking great care of your canine companion throughout his formative and adult years, the transition to senior status should be a smooth one. Age is not a disease, and as long as everything is functioning as it should, there is no reason why most of late adulthood should not be rewarding for both you and your pet. This is especially true if you have tended to the details, such as regular veterinary visits, proper dental care, excellent nutrition and management of bone and joint issues.

At this stage in life, your veterinarian should want to schedule visits twice yearly, instead of once, to run laboratory screenings, electrocardiograms and the like and to change the diet to something more digestible. Catching problems early is the best way to manage them effectively. Treating the early stages of heart disease is so much easier than trying to intervene when there is more significant damage to the heart muscle. Similarly, managing the beginning of kidney problems is fairly routine if there is not significant kidney damage. Other problems, like cognitive dysfunction (similar to senility and Alzheimer's disease), cancer, diabetes and arthritis, are more common in older dogs but all can be treated to help the dog live as many happy, comfortable years as

DENTAL WARNING SIGNS

It is critical to commence regular dental care at home if you have not already done so. It may not sound so important, but most dogs have active periodontal disease by four years of age if they don't have their teeth cleaned regularly at home, not just at their veterinary exams. Dental problems, to which small dogs can be particularly prone, lead to more than just bad "doggy breath." Gum disease can have very serious medical consequences. If you start brushing your dog's teeth and using antiseptic rinses from a young age, your dog will be accustomed to it and will not resist. The results will be healthy dentition, which your pet will need to enjoy a long, healthy life.

possible. Just as in people, medical management is more effective (and less expensive) when you catch things early.

SELECTING A VETERINARIAN

There is probably no more important decision that you will make regarding your pet's health-care than the selection of his doctor. Your pet's veterinarian will be a pediatrician, family-practice physician and gerontolo-gist, depending on the dog's life stage, and will be the individual who makes recommendations regarding issues such as when specialists need to be consulted,

YOUR DOG NEEDS TO VISIT THE VET IF:

- He has ingested a toxin such as antifreeze or a toxic plant; in these cases, administer first aid and call the vet right away
- His teeth are discolored, loose or missing or he has sores or other signs of infection or abnormality in the mouth
- He has been vomiting, has had diarrhea or has been constipated for over 24 hours; call immediately if you notice blood
- He has refused food for over 24 hours
- His eating habits, water intake or toilet habits have noticeably changed; if you have noticed weight gain or weight loss
- He shows symptoms of bloat, which requires *immediate* attention
- He is salivating excessively
- He has a lump in his throat
- He has a lump or bumps anywhere on the body
- He is very lethargic
- He appears to be in pain or otherwise has trouble chewing or swallowing
- His skin loses elasticity

Of course, there will be other instances in which a visit to the vet is necessary; these are just some of the signs that could be indicative of serious problems that need to be caught as early as possible.

when diagnostic testing and/or therapeutic intervention is needed and when you will need to seek outside emergency and critical-care services. Your vet will act as your advocate and liaison throughout these processes.

Everyone has his own idea about what to look for in a vet, an individual who will play a big role in his dog's (and, of course, his own) life for many years to come. For some, it is the compassionate caregiver with whom they hope to develop a professional relationship to span the lives of their dogs and even their future pets. For others, they are seeking a clinician with keen diagnostic and therapeutic insight, who can deliver state-of-the-art healthcare. Still others need a veterinary facility that is open evenings and weekends, is in close proximity or provides mobile veterinary services to accommodate their schedules; these people may not much mind that their dogs might see different veterinarians on each visit. Just as we have different reasons for selecting our own healthcare professionals (e.g., covered by insurance plan, expert in field, convenient location, etc.), we should not expect that there is a one-size-fits-all recommendation for selecting a veterinarian and veterinary practice. The best advice is to be honest in your assessment of what you expect from a veterinary practice and to conscientiously research the options in your area. You will quickly appreciate that all veterinary practices are not the same and you will be happiest with one that truly meets your needs.

There is another point to be considered in the selection of veterinary services. Not that long ago, a single veterinarian would attempt to manage all medical and surgical issues as they arose. That was often problematic, because veterinarians are trained in many species and many diseases, and it was just impossible for general veterinary practitioners to be experts in every species, breed, field and ailment. However, just as in the human healthcare fields, specialization has allowed general practitioners to concentrate on primary healthcare delivery, especially wellness and the prevention of infectious diseases, and to utilize a network of specialists to assist in the management of conditions that require specific expertise and experience. Thus there are now many types of veterinary specialists, including dermatologists, cardiologists, ophthalmologists, surgeons, internists, oncologists, neurolo-

gists, behaviorists, criticalists and others to help primary-care veterinarians deal with complicated medical challenges. In most cases, specialists see cases referred by primary-care veterinarians, make diagnoses and set up management plans. From there, the animals' ongoing care is returned to their primary-care veterinarians. This important team approach to your pet's medical-care needs has provided opportunities for advanced care and an unparalleled level of quality to be delivered.

With all of the opportunities for your pet to receive high-quality veterinary medical care, there is another topic that needs to be addressed at the same time—cost. It's been said that you can have excellent healthcare or inexpensive healthcare but never both; this is as true in veterinary medicine as it is in human medicine. While veterinary costs are a fraction of what the same services cost in the human healthcare arena, it is still difficult to deal with unanticipated medical costs, especially since they can easily creep into hundreds or even thousands of dollars if specialists or emergency services become involved. However, there are ways of managing these risks. The easiest is to buy pet health insurance and realize that its foremost purpose is not to cover routine healthcare visits but rather

COMMON INFECTIOUS DISEASES

Let's discuss some of the diseases that create the need for vaccination in the first place. Following are the major canine infectious diseases and a simple explanation of each.

Rabies: A devastating viral disease that can be fatal in dogs and people. In fact, vaccination of dogs and cats is an important public-health measure to create a resistant animal buffer population to protect people from contracting the disease. Vaccination schedules are determined on a government level and are not optional for pet owners; rabies vaccination is required by law in all 50 states.

Parvovirus: A severe, potentially life-threatening disease that is easily transmitted between dogs. There are four strains of the virus, but it is believed that there is significant "cross-protection" between strains that may be included in individual vaccines.

Distemper: A potentially severe and life-threatening disease with a relatively high risk of exposure, especially in certain regions. In very high-risk distemper environments, young pups may be vaccinated with human measles vaccine, a related virus that offers cross-protection when administered at four to ten weeks of age.

Hepatitis: Caused by canine adenovirus type 1 (CAV-1), but since vaccination with the causative virus has a higher rate of adverse effects, cross-protection is derived from the use of adenovirus type 2 (CAV-2), a cause of respiratory disease and one of the potential causes of canine cough. Vaccination with CAV-2 provides long-term immunity against hepatitis, but relatively less protection against respiratory infection.

Canine cough: Also called tracheobronchitis, actually a fairly complicated result of viral and bacterial offenders; therefore, even with vaccination, protection is incomplete. Wherever dogs congregate, canine cough will likely be spread among them. Intranasal vaccination with *Bordetella* and parainfluenza is the best safeguard, but the duration of immunity does not appear to be very long, typically a year at most. These are non-core vaccines, but vaccination is sometimes mandated by boarding kennels, obedience classes, dog shows and other places where dogs congregate to try to minimize spread of infection.

Leptospirosis: A potentially fatal disease that is more common in some geographic regions. It is capable of being spread to humans. The disease varies with the individual "serovar," or strain, of *Leptospira* involved. Since there does not appear to be much cross-protection between serovars, protection is only as good as the likelihood that the serovar in the vaccine is the same as the one in the pet's local environment. Problems with *Leptospira* vaccines are that protection does not last very long, side effects are not uncommon and a large percentage of dogs (perhaps 30%) may not respond to vaccination.

Borrelia burgdorferi: The cause of Lyme disease, the risk of which varies with the geographic area in which the pet lives and travels. Lyme disease is spread by deer ticks in the eastern US and western black-legged ticks in the western part of the country, and the risk of exposure is high in some regions. Lameness, fever and inappetence are most commonly seen in affected dogs. The extent of protection from the vaccine has not been conclusively demonstrated.

Coronavirus: This disease has a high risk of exposure, especially in areas where dogs congregate, but it typically causes only mild to moderate digestive upset (diarrhea, vomiting, etc.). Vaccines are available, but the duration of protection is believed to be relatively short and the effectiveness of the vaccine in preventing infection is considered low.

There are many other vaccinations available, including those for *Giardia* and canine adenovirus-1. While there may be some specific indications for their use, and local risk factors to be considered, they are not widely recommended for most dogs.

to serve as an umbrella for those rainy days when your pet needs medical care and you don't want to worry about whether or not you can afford that care.

Pet insurance policies are very cost-effective (and very inexpensive by human health-insurance standards), but make sure that you buy the policy long before you intend to use it (preferably starting in puppyhood, because coverage will exclude pre-existing conditions) and that you are actually buying an indemnity insurance plan from an insurance company that is regulated by your state or province. Many insurance policy look-alikes are actually discount clubs that are only redeemable at specific locations and for specific services. An indemnity plan covers your pet at almost all veterinary, specialty and emergency practices and is an excellent way to manage your pet's ongoing healthcare needs.

VACCINATIONS AND INFECTIOUS DISEASES

There has never been an easier time to prevent a variety of infectious diseases in your dog, but these advances come with a price—choice. Now while it may seem that this is a good thing (and it is), it also has never been more difficult for the pet owner (or the vet) to make an informed decision about the best way to protect pets through vaccination.

Years ago, it was just accepted that puppies got a starter series of vaccinations and then annual "boosters" throughout their lives to keep them protected. As more and more vaccines became available, consumers wanted the convenience of having all of that protection in a single injection. The result was "multivalent" vaccines that crammed a lot of protection into a single syringe. The manufacturers' recommendations were to give the vaccines annually, and this was a simple enough protocol to follow. However, as veterinary medicine has become more sophisticated, and we have started looking more at healthcare quandaries rather than convenience, it became necessary to reevaluate the situation and deal with some tough questions. It is important to realize that whether or not to use a particular vaccine depends on the risk of contracting the disease against which it protects, the severity of the disease if it is contracted, the duration of immunity provided by the vaccine, the safety of the product and the needs of the individual animal. In a very general sense, rabies, distemper, hepatitis and parvovirus are considered core vaccine needs, while parain-fluenza, *Bordetella bronchi-septica*, *Leptospira*, coronavirus and borreliosis (Lyme disease) are considered non-core needs and best reserved for animals that demonstrate reasonable risk of contracting the diseases.

NEUTERING/SPAYING

Sterilization procedures (neutering for males/spaying for females) are meant to accomplish several purposes. While the underlying premise is to address the risk of pet overpopulation, there are also some medical and behavioral benefits to the surgeries as well. For females, spaying prior to the first estrus (heat cycle) leads to a marked reduction in the risk of mammary cancer and other serious female health problems. There are also no manifestations of "heat" to attract male dogs nor bleeding in the house. For males, there is prevention of testicular cancer and a reduction in the risk of prostate problems. In both sexes there may be some limited reduction in aggressive behaviors toward other dogs and some diminishing of urine marking, roaming and mounting.

While neutering and spaying do indeed prevent animals from contributing to pet overpopulation, even no-cost and low-cost neutering options have not eliminated the problem. Perhaps one of the main reasons for this is that individuals that intentionally breed their dogs and those that

allow their animals to run at large are the main causes of unwanted offspring. Also, animals in shelters are often there because they were abandoned or relinquished, not because they came from unplanned matings. Neutering/spaying is important, but it should be considered in the context of the real causes of animals' ending up in shelters and eventually being euthanized.

One of the important considerations regarding neutering is that it is a surgical procedure. This sometimes gets lost in discussions of low-cost procedures and commoditization of the process. In females, spaying is specifically referred to as an ovariohysterectomy. In this procedure, a midline incision is made in the abdomen and the entire uterus and both ovaries are surgically removed. While this is a major invasive surgical procedure, it usually has few complications because it is typically performed on young healthy animals. However, it is a major surgery, as any woman who has had a hysterectomy will attest.

In males, neutering has traditionally referred to castration, which involves the surgical removal of both testicles. While still a significant piece of surgery, there is not the abdominal exposure that is required in the female surgery. In addition, there is now a chemical sterilization option, in which a solution is injected into each testicle, leading to atrophy of the sperm-producing cells. This can typically be done under sedation rather than full anesthesia. This is a relatively new approach, and there are not long-term clinical studies yet available.

Neutering/spaying is typically done around six months of age at most veterinary hospitals, although techniques have been pioneered to perform the procedures in animals as young as eight weeks of age. In general, the surgeries on the very young animals are done for the specific reason of sterilizing them before they go to their new homes. This is done in some shelter hospitals for assurance that the animals will definitely not produce any pups. Otherwise, these organizations need to rely on owners to comply with their wishes to have the animals "altered" at a later date, something that does not always happen.

There are some exciting immunocontraceptive "vaccines" currently under development, and there may be a time when contraception in pets will not require surgical procedures. We anxiously await these developments.

TAKING YOUR DOG'S TEMPERATURE

It is important to know how to take your dog's temperature at times when you think he may be ill. It's not the most enjoyable task, but it can be done without too much difficulty. It's easier with a helper, preferably someone with whom the dog is friendly, so that one of you can hold the dog while the other inserts the thermometer.

Before inserting the thermometer, coat the end with petroleum jelly. Insert the thermometer slowly and gently into the dog's rectum about 1 inch. Wait for the reading, about two minutes. Be sure to remove the thermometer carefully and clean it thoroughly after each use.

A dog's normal body temperature is between 100.5 and 102.5 degrees F. Immediate veterinary attention is required if the dog's temperature is below 99 or above 104 degrees F.

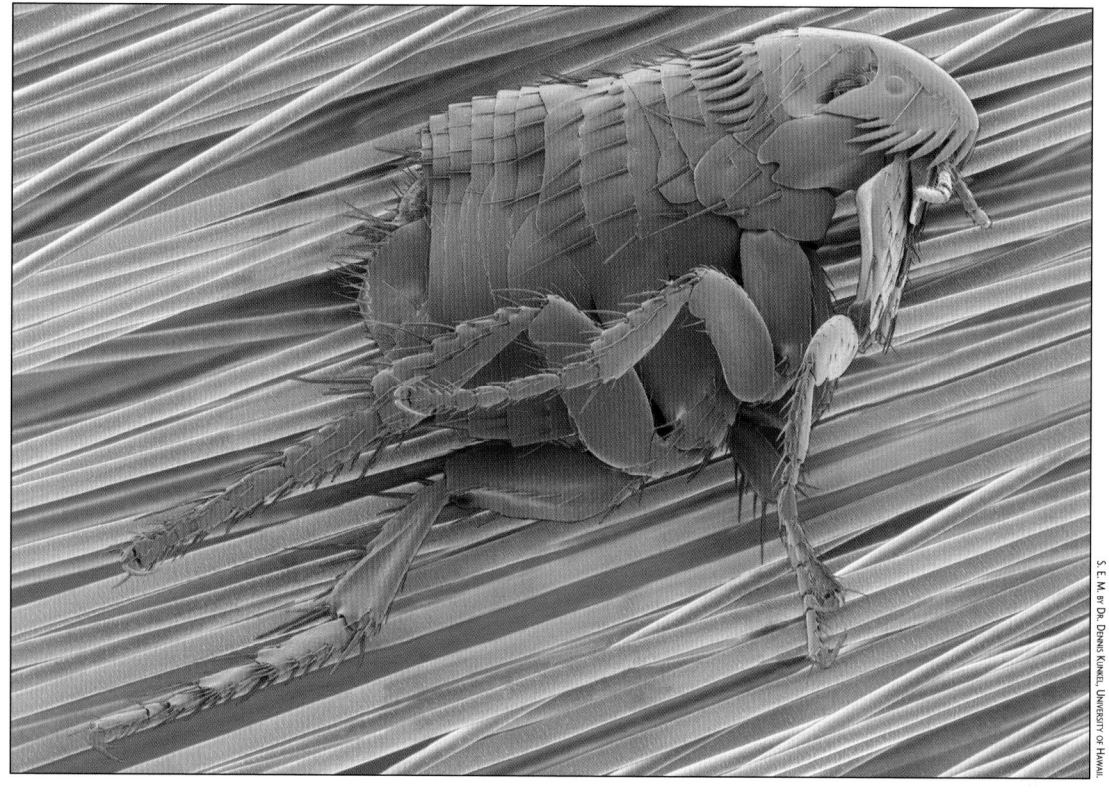

S. E. M. BY DR. DENNIS KUNKEL, UNIVERSITY OF HAWAII

A scanning electron micrograph of a dog flea, *Ctenocephalides canis,* on dog hair.

EXTERNAL PARASITES

FLEAS

Fleas have been around for millions of years and, while we have better tools now for controlling them than at any time in the past, there still is little chance that they will end up on an endangered species list. Actually, they are very well adapted to living on our pets, and they continue to adapt as we make advances.

The female flea can consume 15 times her weight in blood during active reproduction and can lay as many as 40 eggs a day. These eggs are very resistant to the effects of insecticides. They hatch into larvae, which then mature and spin cocoons. The immature fleas reside in this pupal stage until the time is right for feeding. This pupal stage is also very resistant to the effects of insecticides, and pupae can last in the environment without feeding for many months. Newly emergent fleas are attracted to animals by the warmth of the animals' bodies, movement and exhaled carbon dioxide. However, when they first emerge from their cocoons, they orient towards light; thus when an animal passes between a flea and the light source, casting a shadow, the flea pounces and starts to feed. If the animal turns out to be a dog or cat, the reproductive cycle continues. If the flea lands on another type of animal, including a person, the flea will bite but will then look for a more appropriate host. An emerging adult flea can survive without feeding for up to 12 months but, once it tastes blood, it can survive off its host for only 3 to 4 days.

It was once thought that fleas spend most of their lives in the environment, but we now know that fleas won't willingly jump off a dog unless leaping to another dog or when physically removed by brushing, bathing or other manipulation. Flea eggs, on the other hand, are shiny and smooth, and they roll off the animal and into the environment. The eggs, larvae and pupae then exist in the environment, but once the adult finds a susceptible animal, it's home sweet home until the flea is forced to seek refuge elsewhere.

Since adult fleas live on the animal and immature forms survive in the environment, a successful treatment plan must address all stages of the flea life cycle. There are now several safe and effective flea-control products that can be applied on a monthly

---

FLEA PREVENTION FOR YOUR DOG

- Discuss with your veterinarian the safest product to protect your dog, likely in the form of a monthly tablet or a liquid preparation placed on the back of the dog's neck.
- For dogs suffering from flea-bite dermatitis, a shampoo or topical insecticide treatment is required.
- Your lawn and property should be sprayed with an insecticide designed to kill fleas and ticks that lurk outdoors.
- Using a flea comb, check the dog's coat regularly for any signs of parasites.
- Practice good housekeeping. Vacuum floors, carpets and furniture regularly, especially in the areas that the dog frequents, and wash the dog's bedding weekly.
- Follow up house-cleaning with carpet shampoos and sprays to rid the house of fleas at all stages of development. Insect growth regulators are the safest option.

---

basis. These include fipronil, imidacloprid, selamectin and permethrin (found in several formulations). Most of these products have significant flea-killing rates within 24 hours. However, none of them will control the immature forms in the environment. To accomplish this, there are a variety of insect growth regulators that can be

THE FLEA'S LIFE CYCLE

What came first, the flea or the egg? This age-old mystery is more difficult to comprehend than the actual cycle of the flea. Fleas usually live only about four months. A female can lay 2,000 eggs in her lifetime.

Egg

PHOTO BY CAROLINA BIOLOGICAL SUPPLY CO.

After ten days of rolling around your carpet or under your furniture, the eggs hatch into larvae, which feed on various and sundry debris. In days or months, depending on the climate, the larvae spin cocoons and develop into the pupal or nymph stage, which quickly develop into fleas.

Larva

PHOTO BY CAROLINA BIOLOGICAL SUPPLY CO.

Pupa

These immature fleas must locate a host within 10 to 14 days or they will die. Only about 1% of the flea population exist as adult fleas, while the other 99% exist as eggs, larvae or pupae.

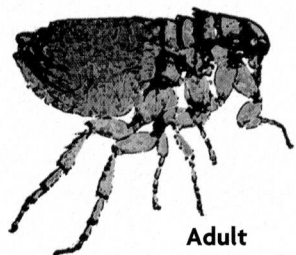

Adult

KILL FLEAS THE NATURAL WAY

If you choose not to go the route of conventional medication, there are some natural ways to ward off fleas:

- Dust your dog with a natural flea powder, composed of such herbal goodies as rosemary, wormwood, pennyroyal, citronella, rue, tobacco powder and eucalyptus.
- Apply diatomaceous earth, the fossilized remains of single-cell algae, to your carpets, furniture and pet's bedding. Even though it's not good for dogs, it's even worse for fleas, which will dry up swiftly and die.
- Brush your dog frequently, give him adequate exercise and let him fast occasionally. All of these activities strengthen the dog's immune system and make him more resistant to disease and parasites.
- Bathe your dog with a capful of pennyroyal or eucalyptus oil.
- Feed a natural diet, free of additives and preservatives. Add some fresh garlic and brewer's yeast to the dog's morning portion, as these items have flea-repelling properties.

sprayed into the environment (e.g., pyriproxyfen, methoprene, fenoxycarb) as well as insect development inhibitors such as lufenuron that can be administered. These compounds have no effect on adult fleas, but they stop immature forms from developing into adults. In years gone by, we relied heavily on toxic insecticides (such as organophosphates, organochlorines and carbamates) to manage the flea problem, but today's options are not only much safer to use on our pets but also safer for the environment.

TICKS

Ticks are members of the spider class (arachnids) and are blood-sucking parasites capable of transmitting a variety of diseases, including Lyme disease, ehrlichiosis, babesiosis and Rocky Mountain spotted fever. It's easy to see ticks on your own skin, but it is more of a challenge when your furry companion is affected. Whenever you happen to be planning a stroll in a tick-infested area (especially forests, grassy or wooded areas or parks) be prepared to do a thorough inspection of your dog afterward to search for ticks. Ticks can be tricky, so make sure you spend time looking in the ears, between the toes and everywhere else where a tick might hide. Ticks need to be attached for 24–72 hours before they transmit most of the diseases that they carry, so you do have a window of opportunity for some preventive intervention.

A TICKING BOMB

There is nothing good about a tick's harpooning his nose into your dog's skin. Among the diseases caused by ticks are Rocky Mountain spotted fever, canine ehrlichiosis, canine babesiosis, canine hepatozoonosis and Lyme disease. If a dog is allergic to the saliva of a female wood tick, he can develop tick paralysis.

S. E. M. BY PHOTOTAKE.

A scanning electron micrograph of the head of a female deer tick, *Ixodes dammini,* a parasitic tick that carries Lyme disease.

Female ticks live to eat and breed. They can lay between 4,000 and 5,000 eggs and they die soon after. Males, on the other hand, live only to mate with the females and continue the process as long as they are able. Most ticks live on multiple hosts before parasitizing dogs. The immature forms typically reside on grass and shrubs, waiting for suscep-tible animals to walk by. The larvae and nymph stages typically feed on wildlife.

If only a few ticks are present on a dog, they can be plucked out, but it is important to remove the entire head and mouthparts,

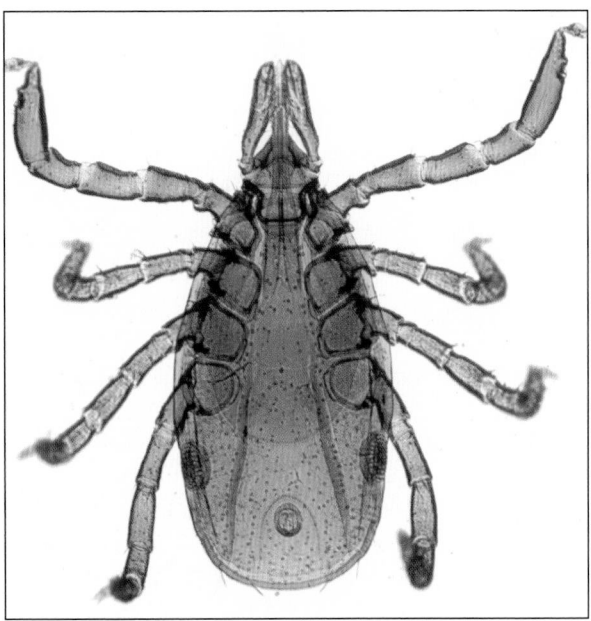

Photo by Carolina Biological Supply Co.

Deer tick,
Ixodes dammini.

which may be deeply embedded in the skin. This is best accomplished with forceps designed especially for this purpose; fingers can be used but should be protected with rubber gloves, plastic wrap or at least a paper towel. The tick should be grasped as closely as possible to the animal's skin and should be pulled upward with steady, even pressure. Do not squeeze, crush or puncture the body of the tick or you risk exposure to any disease carried by that tick. Once the ticks have been removed, the sites of attachment should be disinfected. Your hands should then be washed with soap and water to further minimize risk of contagion. The tick should be

disposed of in a container of alcohol or household bleach.

Some of the newer flea products, specifically those with fipronil, selamectin and permethrin, have effect against some, but not all, species of tick. Flea collars containing appropriate pesticides (e.g., propoxur, chlorfenvinphos) can aid in tick control. In most areas, such collars should be placed on animals in March, at the beginning of the tick season, and changed regularly. Leaving the collar on when the pesticide level is waning invites the development of resistance. Amitraz collars are also good for tick control, and the active ingredient does not interfere with other flea-control products. The ingredient helps prevent the attachment of ticks to the skin and will cause those ticks already on the skin to detach themselves.

TICK CONTROL

Removal of underbrush and leaf litter and the thinning of trees in areas where tick control is desired are recommended. These actions remove the cover and food sources for small animals that serve as hosts for ticks. With continued mowing of grasses in these areas, the probability of ticks' surviving is further reduced. A variety of insecticide ingredients (e.g., resmethrin, carbaryl, permethrin, chlorpyrifos, dioxathion and allethrin) are registered for tick control around the home.

MITES

Mites are tiny arachnid parasites that parasitize the skin of dogs. Skin diseases caused by mites are referred to as "mange," and there are many different forms seen in dogs. These forms are very different from one another, each one warranting an individual description.

Sarcoptic mange, or scabies, is one of the itchiest conditions that affects dogs. The microscopic *Sarcoptes* mites burrow into the superficial layers of the skin and can drive dogs crazy with itchiness. They are also communicable to people, although they can't complete their reproductive cycle on people. In addition to being tiny, the mites also are often difficult to find when trying to make a diagnosis. Skin scrapings from multiple areas are examined microscopically but, even then, sometimes the mites cannot be found.

Fortunately, scabies is relatively easy to treat, and there are a variety of products that will successfully kill the mites. Since the mites can't live in the environment for very long without feeding, a complete cure is usually possible within four to eight weeks.

Cheyletiellosis is caused by a relatively large mite, which sometimes can be seen even without a microscope. Often referred to as "walking dandruff," this also causes itching, but not usually as profound as with scabies. While *Cheyletiella*

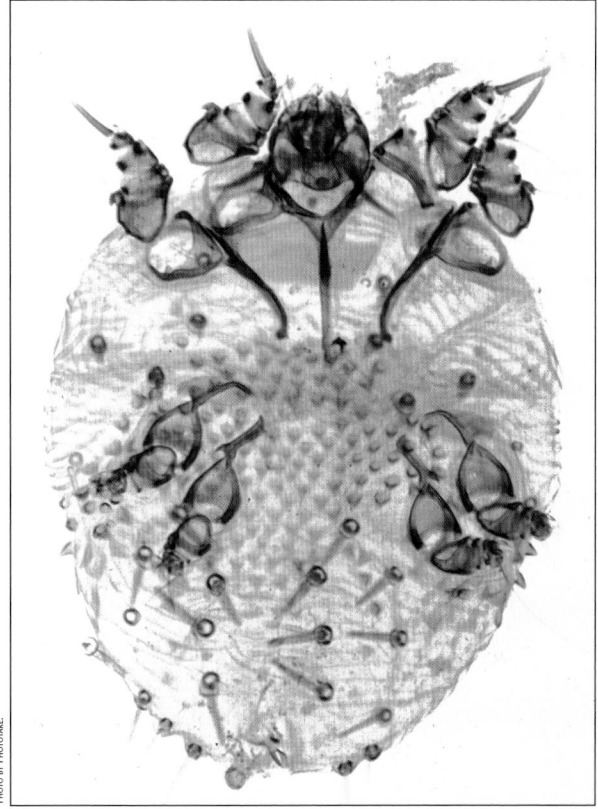

PHOTO BY PHOTOTAKE.

Sarcoptes scabiei, commonly known as the "itch mite."

mites can survive somewhat longer in the environment than scabies mites, they too are relatively easy to treat, being responsive to not only the medications used to treat scabies but also often to flea-control products.

Otodectes cynotis is the canine ear mite and is one of the more common causes of mange, especially in young dogs in shelters or pet stores. That's because the mites are typically present in large numbers and are quickly spread to nearby animals. The mites rarely do

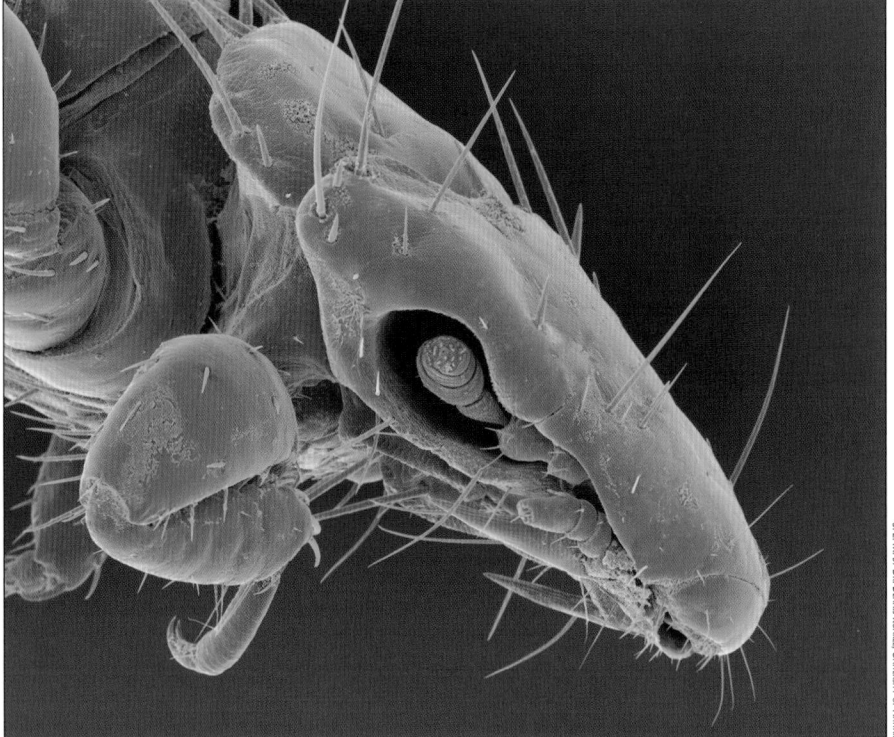

Micrograph of a dog louse, *Heterodoxus spiniger.* Female lice attach their eggs to the hairs of the dog. As the eggs hatch, the larval lice bite and feed on the blood. Lice can also feed on dead skin and hair. This feeding activity can cause hair loss and skin problems.

S. E. M. BY DR. DENNIS KUNKEL, UNIVERSITY OF HAWAII.

much harm but can be difficult to eradicate if the treatment regimen is not comprehensive. While many try to treat the condition with ear drops only, this is the most common cause of treatment failure. Ear drops cause the mites to simply move out of the ears and as far away as possible (usually to the base of the tail) until the insecticide levels in the ears drop to an acceptable level—then it's back to business as usual! The successful treatment of ear mites requires treating all animals in the household with a systemic insecticide, such as selamectin, or a combination of miticidal ear drops

combined with whole-body flea-control preparations.

Demodicosis, sometimes referred to as red mange, can be one of the most difficult forms of mange to treat. Part of the problem has to do with the fact that the mites live in the hair follicles and they are relatively well shielded from topical and systemic products. The main issue, however, is that demodectic mange typically results only when there is some underlying process interfering with the dog's immune system.

Since *Demodex* mites are normal residents of the skin of

mammals, including humans, there is usually a mite population explosion only when the immune system fails to keep the number of mites in check. In young animals, the immune deficit may be transient or may reflect an actual inherited immune problem. In older animals, demodicosis is usually seen only when there is another disease hampering the immune system, such as diabetes, cancer, thyroid problems or the use of immune-suppressing drugs. Accordingly, treatment involves not only trying to kill the mange mites but also discerning what is interfering with immune function and correcting it if possible.

Chiggers represent several different species of mite that don't parasitize dogs specifically, but do latch on to passersby and can cause irritation. The problem is most prevalent in wooded areas in the late summer and fall. Treatment is not difficult, as the mites do not complete their life cycle on dogs and are susceptible to a variety of miticidal products.

MOSQUITOES
Mosquitoes have long been known to transmit a variety of diseases to people, as well as just being biting pests during warm weather. They also pose a real risk to pets. Not only do they carry deadly heartworms

but recently there also has been much concern over their involvement with West Nile virus. While we can avoid heartworm with the use of preventive medications, there are no such preventives for West Nile virus. The only method of prevention in endemic areas is active mosquito control. Fortunately, most dogs that have been exposed to the virus only developed flu-like symptoms and, to date, there have not been the large number of reported deaths in canines as seen in some other species.

Illustration of *Demodex folliculoram.*

MOSQUITO REPELLENT
Low concentrations of DEET (less than 10%), found in many human mosquito repellents, have been safely used in dogs but, in these concentrations, probably give only about two hours of protection. DEET may be safe in these small concentrations, but since it is not licensed for use on dogs, there is no research proving its safety for dogs. Products containing permethrin give the longest-lasting protection, perhaps two to four weeks. As DEET is not licensed for use on dogs, and both DEET and permethrin can be quite toxic to cats, appropriate care should be exercised. Other products, such as those containing oil of citronella, also have some mosquito-repellent activity, but typically have a relatively short duration of action.

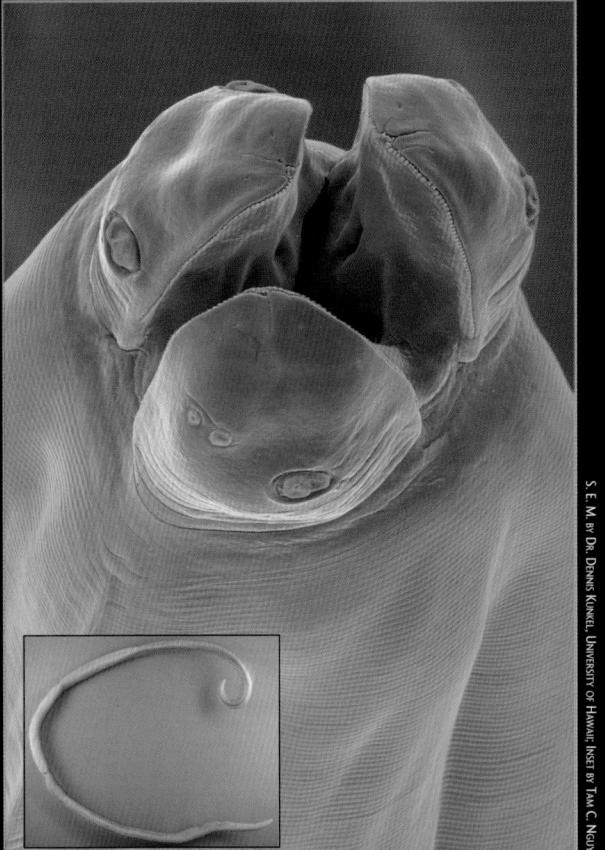

The ascarid roundworm *Toxocara canis*, showing the mouth with three lips. INSET: Photomicrograph of the roundworm *Ascaris lumbricoides*.

ASCARID DANGERS

The most commonly encountered worms in dogs are roundworms known as ascarids. *Toxascaris leonine* and *Toxocara canis* are the two species that infect dogs. Subsisting in the dog's stomach and intestines, adult roundworms can grow to 7 inches in length and adult females can lay in excess of 200,000 eggs in a single day.

In humans, visceral larval migrans affects people who have ingested eggs of *Toxocara canis*, which frequently contaminates children's sandboxes, beaches and park grounds. The roundworms reside in the human's stomach and intestines, as they would in a dog's, but do not mature. Instead, they find their way to the liver, lungs and skin, or even to the heart or kidneys in severe cases. Deworming puppies is critical in preventing the infection in humans, and young children should never handle nursing pups who have not been dewormed.

INTERNAL PARASITES: WORMS

ASCARIDS

Ascarids are intestinal roundworms that rarely cause severe disease in dogs. Nonetheless, they are of major public health significance because they can be transferred to people. Sadly, it is children who are most commonly affected by the parasite, probably from inadvertently ingesting ascarid-contaminated soil. In fact, many yards and children's sandboxes contain appreciable numbers of ascarid eggs. So, while ascarids don't bite dogs or latch onto their intestines to suck blood, they do cause some nasty medical conditions in children and are best eradicated from our furry friends. Because pups can start passing ascarid eggs by three weeks of age, most parasite-control programs begin at two weeks of age and are repeated every two weeks until pups are eight weeks old. It is important to

HOOKED ON ANCYLOSTOMA

Adult dogs can become infected by the bloodsucking nematodes we commonly call hookworms via ingesting larvae from the ground or via the larvae penetrating the dog's skin. It is not uncommon for infected dogs to show no symptoms of hookworm infestation. Sometimes symptoms occur within ten days of exposure. These symptoms can include bloody diarrhea, anemia, loss of weight and general weakness. Dogs pass the hookworm eggs in their stools, which serves as the vet's method of identifying the infestation. The hookworm larvae can encyst themselves in the dog's tissues and be released when the dog is experiencing stress.

Caused by an *Ancylostoma* species whose common host is the dog, cutaneous larval migrans affects humans, causing itching and lumps and streaks beneath the surface of the skin.

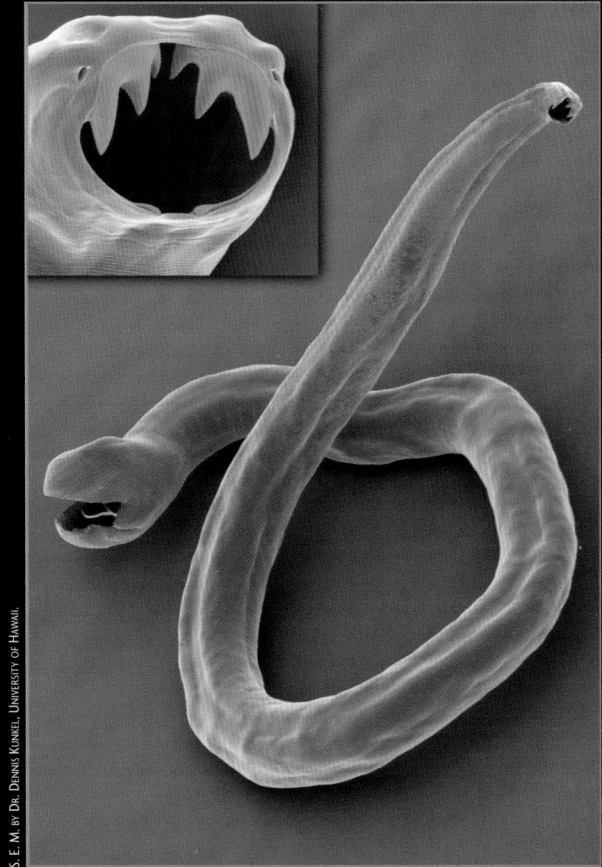

S. E. M. by Dr. Dennis Kunkel, University of Hawaii.

realize that bitches can pass ascarids to their pups even if they test negative prior to whelping. Accordingly, bitches are best treated at the same time as the pups.

HOOKWORMS

Unlike ascarids, hookworms do latch onto a dog's intestinal tract and can cause significant loss of blood and protein. Similar to ascarids, hookworms can be transmitted to humans, where they cause a condition known as cutaneous larval migrans. Dogs can become infected either by consuming the infective larvae or by the larvae's penetrating the skin directly. People most often get infected when they are lying on the ground (such as on a beach) and the larvae penetrate the skin. Yes, the larvae can penetrate through a beach blanket. Hookworms are typically susceptible to the same medications used to treat ascarids.

The hookworm *Ancylostoma caninum* infests the intestines of dogs. INSET: Note the row of hooks at the posterior end, used to anchor the worm to the intestinal wall.

WHIPWORMS

Whipworms latch onto the lower aspects of the dog's colon and can cause cramping and diarrhea. Eggs do not start to appear in the dog's feces until about three months after the dog was infected. This worm has a peculiar life cycle, which makes it more difficult to control than ascarids or hookworms. The good thing is that whipworms rarely are transferred to people.

Some of the medications used to treat ascarids and hookworms are also effective against whipworms, but, in general, a separate treatment protocol is needed. Since most of the medications are effective against the adults but not the eggs or larvae, treatment is typically repeated in three weeks, and then often in three

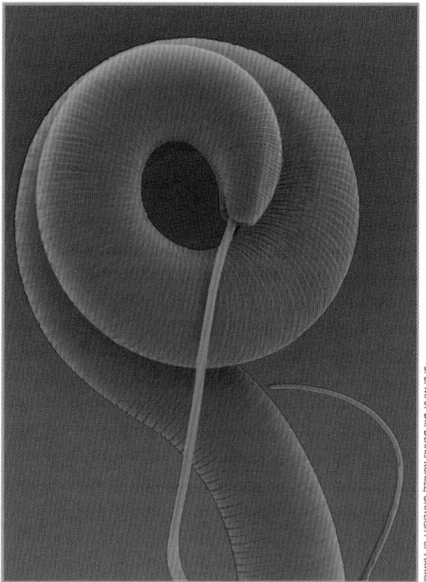

Adult whipworm, *Trichuris* sp., an intestinal parasite.

S.E.M. BY DR. DENNIS KUNKEL, UNIVERSITY OF HAWAII

WORM-CONTROL GUIDELINES

- Practice sanitary habits with your dog and home.
- Clean up after your dog and don't let him sniff or eat other dogs' droppings.
- Control insects and fleas in the dog's environment. Fleas, lice, cockroaches, beetles, mice and rats can act as hosts for various worms.
- Prevent dogs from eating uncooked meat, raw poultry and dead animals.
- Keep dogs and children from playing in sand and soil.
- Kennel dogs on cement or gravel; avoid dirt runs.
- Administer heartworm preventives regularly.
- Have your vet examine your dog's stool at your annual visits.
- Select a boarding kennel carefully so as to avoid contamination from other dogs or an unsanitary environment.
- Prevent dogs from roaming. Obey local leash laws.

months as well. Unfortunately, since dogs don't develop resistance to whipworms, it is difficult to prevent them from getting reinfected if they visit soil contaminated with whipworm eggs.

TAPEWORMS

There are many different species of tapeworm that affect dogs, but *Dipylidium caninum* is probably the most common and is spread by fleas. Flea larvae feed on organic debris and tapeworm eggs in the environment and, when a dog chews at himself and manages to ingest fleas, he might get a dose of tapeworm at the same time. The tapeworm then develops further in the intestine of the dog.

The tapeworm itself, which is a parasitic flatworm that latches onto the intestinal wall, is composed of numerous segments. When the segments break off into the intestine (as proglottids), they may accumulate around the rectum, like grains of rice. While this tapeworm is disgusting in its behavior, it is not directly communicable to humans (although humans can also get infected by swallowing fleas).

A much more dangerous tapeworm is *Echinococcus multilocularis*, which is typically found in foxes, coyotes and wolves. The eggs are passed in the feces and infect rodents, and, when dogs eat the rodents, the dogs can be infected by thousands of adult tapeworms. While the parasites don't cause many problems in dogs, this is considered the most lethal worm infection that people can get. Take appropriate precautions if you live in an area in which these tapeworms are found. Do not use mulch that may contain feces of dogs, cats or wildlife, and

discourage your pets from hunting wildlife. Treat these tapeworm infections aggressively in pets, because if humans get infected, approximately half die.

HEARTWORMS
Heartworm disease is caused by the parasite *Dirofilaria immitis* and is seen in dogs around the world. A member of the roundworm group, it is spread between dogs by the bite of an infected mosquito. The mosquito injects infective larvae into the dog's skin with its bite, and these larvae develop under the skin for a period of time before making their way to the heart. There they develop into adults, which grow and create blockages of the heart, lungs and major blood vessels there. They also start producing offspring (microfilariae),

A dog tapeworm proglottid (body segment).

The dog tapeworm *Taenia pisiformis*.

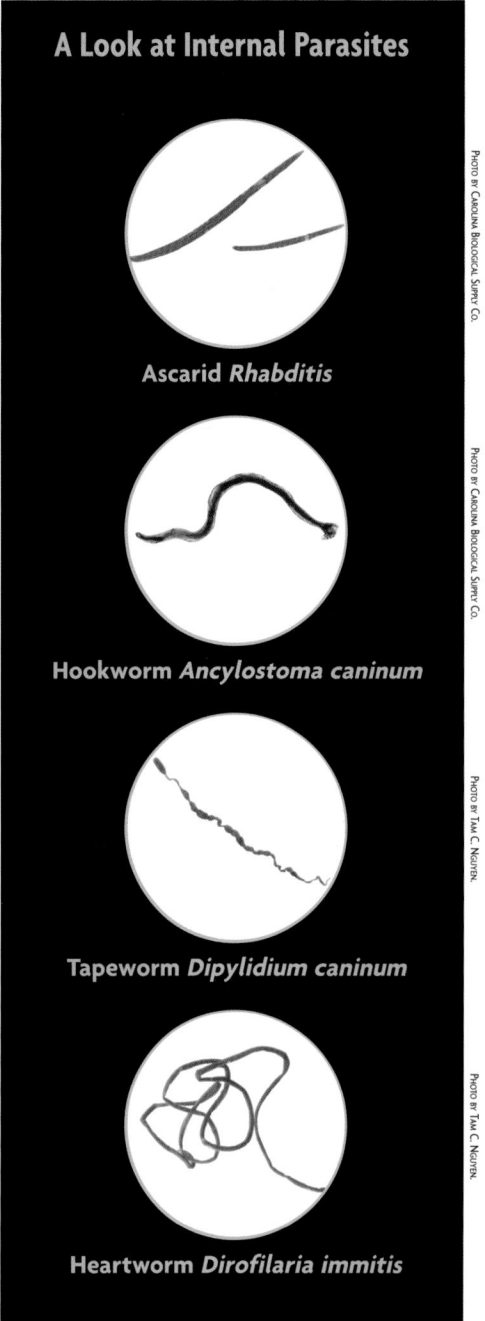

A Look at Internal Parasites

Ascarid *Rhabditis*

Hookworm *Ancylostoma caninum*

Tapeworm *Dipylidium caninum*

Heartworm *Dirofilaria immitis*

PHOTO BY CAROLINA BIOLOGICAL SUPPLY CO.

PHOTO BY CAROLINA BIOLOGICAL SUPPLY CO.

PHOTO BY TAM C. NGUYEN

PHOTO BY TAM C. NGUYEN

and these microfilariae circulate in the bloodstream, waiting to hitch a ride when the next mosquito bites. Once in the mosquito, the microfilariae develop into infective larvae and the entire process is repeated.

When dogs get infected with heartworm, over time they tend to develop symptoms associated with heart disease, such as coughing, exercise intolerance and potentially many other manifestations. Diagnosis is confirmed by either seeing the microfilariae themselves in blood samples or using immunologic tests (antigen testing) to identify the presence of adult heartworms. Since antigen tests measure the presence of adult heartworms and microfilarial tests measure offspring produced by adults, neither are positive until six to seven months after the initial infection. However, the beginning of damage can occur by fifth-stage larvae as early as three months after infection. Thus it is possible for dogs to be harboring problem-causing larvae for up to three months before either type of test would identify an infection.

The good news is that there are great protocols available for preventing heartworm in dogs. Testing is critical in the process, and it is important to understand the benefits as well as the limitations of such testing. All dogs six months of age or older that have not been on continuous heartworm-preventive medication should be

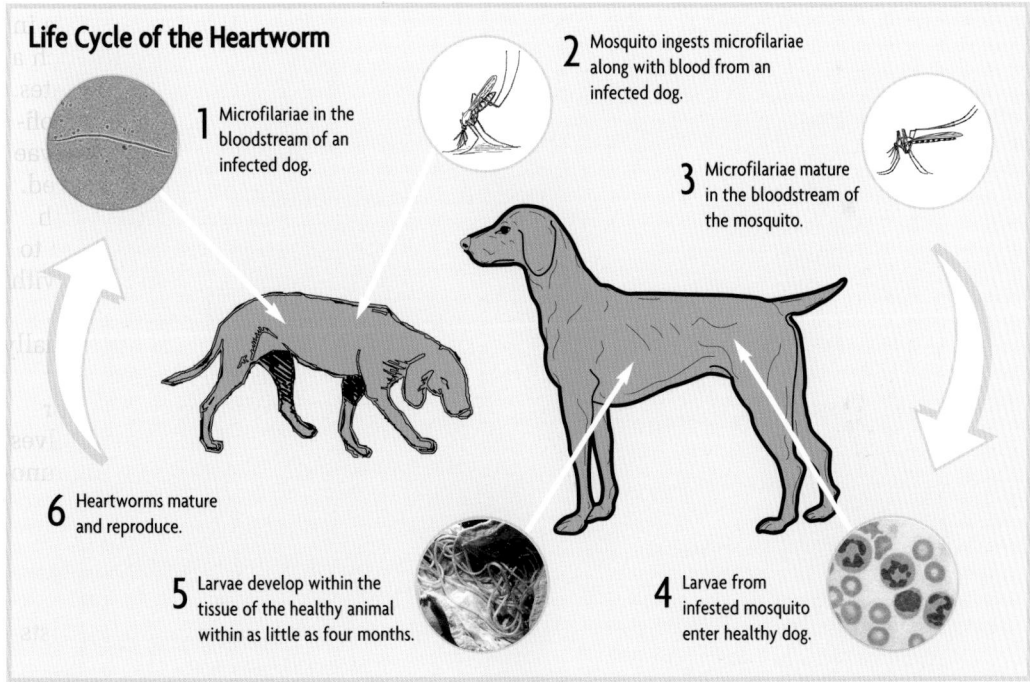

Life Cycle of the Heartworm

1 Microfilariae in the bloodstream of an infected dog.

2 Mosquito ingests microfilariae along with blood from an infected dog.

3 Microfilariae mature in the bloodstream of the mosquito.

4 Larvae from infested mosquito enter healthy dog.

5 Larvae develop within the tissue of the healthy animal within as little as four months.

6 Heartworms mature and reproduce.

screened with microfilarial or antigen tests. For dogs receiving preventive medication, periodic antigen testing helps assess the effectiveness of the preventives. The American Heartworm Society guidelines suggest that annual retesting may not be necessary when owners have absolutely provided continuous heartworm prevention. Retesting on a two- to three-year interval may be sufficient in these cases. However, your veterinarian will likely have specific guidelines under which heartworm preventives will be prescribed, and many prefer to err on the side of safety and retest annually.

It is indeed fortunate that heartworm is relatively easy to prevent, because treatments can be as life-threatening as the disease itself. Treatment requires a two-step process that kills the adult heartworms first and then the microfilariae. Prevention is obviously preferable; this involves a once-monthly oral or topical treatment. The most common oral preventives include ivermectin (not suitable for some breeds), moxidectin and milbemycin oxime; the once-a-month topical drug selamectin provides heartworm protection in addition to flea, some types of tick and other parasite controls.

Number-One Killer Disease in Dogs: CANCER

In every age, there is a word associated with a disease or plague that causes humans to shudder. In the 21st century, that word is "cancer." Just as cancer is the leading cause of death in humans, it claims nearly half the lives of dogs that die from a natural disease as well as half the dogs that die over the age of ten years.

Described as a genetic disease, cancer becomes a greater risk as the dog ages. Vets and dog owners have become increasingly aware of the threat of cancer to dogs. Statistics reveal that one dog in every five will develop cancer, the most common of which is skin cancer. Many cancers, including prostate, ovarian and breast cancer, can be avoided by spaying and neutering our dogs by the age of six months.

Early detection of cancer can save or extend a dog's life, so it is absolutely vital for owners to have their dogs examined by a qualified vet or oncologist immediately upon detection of any abnormality. Certain dietary guidelines have also proven to reduce the onset and spread of cancer. Foods based on fish rather than beef, due to the presence of Omega-3 fatty acids, are recommended. Other amino acids such as glutamine have significant benefits for canines, particularly those breeds that show a greater susceptibility to cancer.

Cancer management and treatments promise hope for future generations of canines. Since the disease is genetic, breeders should never breed a dog whose parents, grandparents and any related siblings have developed cancer. It is difficult to know whether to exclude an otherwise healthy dog from a breeding program, as the disease does not manifest itself until the dog's senior years.

RECOGNIZE CANCER WARNING SIGNS

Since early detection can possibly rescue your dog from becoming a cancer statistic, it is essential for owners to recognize the possible signs and seek the assistance of a qualified professional.

- Abnormal bumps or lumps that continue to grow
- Bleeding or discharge from any body cavity
- Persistent stiffness or lameness
- Recurrent sores or sores that do not heal
- Inappetence
- Breathing difficulties
- Weight loss
- Bad breath or odors
- General malaise and fatigue
- Eating and swallowing problems
- Difficulty urinating and defecating

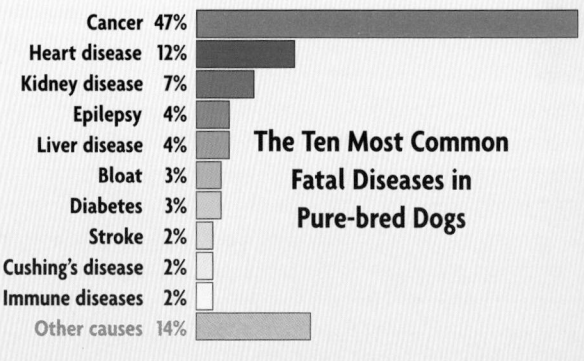

Cancer	47%
Heart disease	12%
Kidney disease	7%
Epilepsy	4%
Liver disease	4%
Bloat	3%
Diabetes	3%
Stroke	2%
Cushing's disease	2%
Immune diseases	2%
Other causes	14%

The Ten Most Common Fatal Diseases in Pure-bred Dogs

CDS: Cognitive Dysfunction Syndrome

"Old-Dog Syndrome"

There are many ways for you to evaluate old-dog syndrome. Veterinarians have defined CDS (cognitive dysfunction syndrome) as the gradual deterioration of cognitive abilities, indicated by changes in the dog's behavior. When a dog changes his routine response, and maladies have been eliminated as the cause of these behavioral changes, then CDS is the usual diagnosis.

More than half the dogs over eight years old suffer from some form of CDS. The older the dog, the more chance he has of suffering from CDS. In humans, doctors often dismiss the CDS behavioral changes as part of "winding down."

There are four major signs of CDS: frequent potty accidents inside the home, sleeping much more or much less than normal, acting confused and failing to respond to social stimuli.

Symptoms of CDS

FREQUENT POTTY ACCIDENTS
- Urinates in the house.
- Defecates in the house.
- Doesn't signal that he wants to go out.

FAILURE TO RESPOND TO SOCIAL STIMULI
- Comes to people less frequently, whether called or not.
- Doesn't tolerate petting for more than a short time.
- Doesn't come to the door when you return home.

CONFUSION
- Goes outside and just stands there.
- Appears confused with a faraway look in his eyes.
- Hides more often.
- Doesn't recognize friends.
- Doesn't come when called.
- Walks around listlessly and without a destination.

SLEEP PATTERNS
- Awakens more slowly.
- Sleeps more than normal during the day.
- Sleeps less during the night.

BOLOGNESE

Beauty is surely not everything, but every owner of a first-rate Bolognese will likely be tempted to have his dog compete at least once at a dog show. A dog show not only is an opportunity to present a dog but also serves to publicize the breeding results for a particular breed. Every dog entered at a show will be judged not only as to his overall quality but also with regard to his appearance and comportment by qualified ring judges. The judge's task is to compare every specimen entered against the standard for the given breed. There is no such thing as the perfect dog, but the closer a Bolognese comes to the imagined ideal, the higher the judge's opinion of that dog should be.

Judging is done with the dog in a standing position ("stacked"). In the case of such a small breed as the Bolognese, the hands-on examination is done on a judging table. Further evaluation is done with the dog in motion, watching his gait, the carriage of his body and tail and his general appearance. All of these aspects are scrutinized in detail. The condition of the dog when he appears in the ring is of major importance.

The aim of dog shows is to identify those dogs that come closest to the standards of their breed and thus show how close breeders have managed to come to the ideal. In this regard, it must not be overlooked that dog shows are extremely effective advertising, giving potential owners an opportunity to make a

Skilled handlers know the best way to "stack," or stand, their dogs in a manner that will show them off to their best advantage for the judge's review.

Small dogs like the Bolognese are placed on a raised table for a thorough hands-on evaluation by the judge.

sensible choice about their future companions. Breeders will be only too happy to answer questions about the qualities of their Bolognese. The future owner, on the other hand, will benefit from the knowledge he can gather about the characteristics of the breed in order to evaluate its suitability for his individual situation and expectations. If you want to show your Bolognese competitively, or if you want to acquire a dog with show qualities, you should also be prepared to invest the necessary patience, time and money, as success will otherwise only be modest if at all.

A dog that is intended to participate successfully in shows on a regular basis must obviously be of high quality. Just as importantly, he has to be prepared for the show ring through regular training. Besides effective grooming, conditioning and show training, both dog and owner must enjoy everything associated with showing in order to be successful.

As a prerequisite, your dog must be suitable for being shown (without any disqualifying or eliminating faults). In order for him to be successful, he must be prepared for a show well in

advance. Training can be done at home or at a training facility that is set up similarly to a show ring. Show training should commence at a very young age, ideally very soon after the pup comes home. Initially, five minutes of training will be enough, with an increase in duration and intensity as the dog grows older. The handler must always ensure that his Bolognese is not unduly stressed in the process, as he may otherwise start to dislike the training.

One of the things a show dog must do is walk properly on leash, which means that the dog stays on the left side of the handler and walks at exactly the handler's speed. The tail and head should be carried with discernible pride. Walking nicely is, however, not all the Bolognese has to learn to present himself with maximum effect. A major aspect of the dog's presentation is how he looks while standing still. For this purpose, the dog is stacked in the proper position both on a table and on the ground. The dog must be taught to present himself in all his beauty. The tail should hang over the back and the head should be raised in a show of self-confidence. He should be still like a statue and exude the personality that a Bolognese is supposed to embody.

The result of all efforts is a show of unity between handler and dog in the ring. Spectators will be fascinated and impressed by a proud and noble Bolognese that quite obviously feels like a king in the show ring and behaves like a professional. Likewise a handler who unobtrusively presents his dog in the best way possible is well appreciated. However, even a top-class show dog will not necessarily finish in first place every time. Every owner should be aware of the shortcomings of his dog, the

strengths of the other dogs and the variation in tasks among the different judges. A dog show should be understood as a competitive sport, in which participating is more important than winning.

A very important aspect is that there are some dogs that just do not like participating in shows. The owner should therefore show his "dog sense" and refrain from forcing his Bolognese to enter this type of competition. It is highly unlikely in such a case that the dog would reach the success that the owner hopes for. Such a Bolognese will in any case

The judge goes over the entire dog to make sure that under the heavy coat is a properly constructed Bolognese.

become your personal treasure, even without titles and certificates, as the main attraction of your family. Not every Bolognese is born to be a star in the ring, but every Bolognese is born to be a star to his owner.

GETTING INTO SHOWING
Is dog showing in your blood? Are you excited by the idea of gaiting your handsome Bolognese around the ring to the thunderous

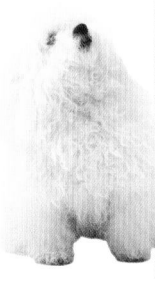

FOR MORE INFORMATION...
For reliable up-to-date information about registration, dog shows and other canine competitions, contact one of the national registries by mail or via the Internet.

Fédération Cynologique Internationale
14, rue Leopold II, B-6530 Thuin, Belgium
www.fci.be

United Kennel Club
100 E. Kilgore Road, Kalamazoo, MI 49002
www.ukcdogs.com

American Rare Breed Association
9921 Frank Tippett Road, Cheltenham, MD 20623
www.arba.org

Canadian Kennel Club
89 Skyway Ave., Suite 100, Etobicoke, Ontario
M9W 6R4, Canada
www.ckc.ca

The Kennel Club
1-5 Clarges St., Piccadilly, London
W1Y 8AB, UK
www.the-kennel-club.org.uk

applause of an enthusiastic audience? Are you certain that your beloved Bolognese is flawless? You are not alone! Every loving owner thinks that his dog has no faults, or too few to mention. No matter how many times an owner reads over the breed standard, he cannot find any faults in his aristocratic companion dog. If this sounds like you, and if you are considering entering your Bolognese in a dog show, here are some basic questions to ask yourself:

• Did you purchase a "show-quality" puppy from the breeder?
• Is your puppy old enough to show?
• Does the puppy exhibit correct show type for his breed?
• Does your puppy have any disqualifying faults?
• Is your Bolognese registered with the appropriate club or organization?
• How much time do you have to devote to training, grooming, conditioning and exhibiting your dog?
• Do you understand the rules and regulations of a dog show?
• Do you have time to learn to how to show your dog properly?
• Do you have the financial resources to invest in showing your dog?
• Will you show the dog yourself or hire a professional handler (if permissible)?

CANINE GOOD CITIZEN® PROGRAM

Have you ever considered getting your dog "certified"? The AKC's Canine Good Citizen® Program affords your dog just that opportunity. Your dog shows that he is a well-behaved canine citizen, using the basic training and good manners you have taught him, by taking a series of ten tests that illustrate that he can behave properly at home, in a public place and around other dogs. The tests are administered by participating dog clubs, colleges, 4-H clubs, Scouts and other community groups and are open to all pure-bred (not just those recognized by the AKC) and mixed-breed dogs. Upon passing the ten tests, the suffix CGC is then applied to your dog's name.

The ten tests are: 1. Accepting a friendly stranger; 2. Sitting politely for petting; 3. Appearance and grooming; 4. Walking on a lead; 5. Walking through a group of people; 6. Sit, down and stay on command; 7. Coming when called; 8. Meeting another dog; 9. Calm reaction to distractions; 10. Separation from owner.

• Do you have a vehicle that can accommodate your weekend trips to the dog shows?

Success in the show ring requires more than a pretty three-buttoned face, a waggy tail and a pocketful of liver. Even though dog shows can be exciting and enjoyable, the sport of conformation makes great demands on the exhibitors and the dogs. Winning exhibitors live for their dogs, devoting time and money to their dogs' presentation, conditioning and training. Very few novices, even those with good dogs, will find themselves in the winners' circle, though it does happen. Don't be disheartened, though. Every exhibitor began as a novice and worked his way up to the Group ring. It's the "working your way up" part that you must keep in mind.

Assuming that you have purchased a puppy of the correct type and quality for showing, let's begin to examine the world of showing and what's required to get started. Although the entry fee into a dog show is nominal, there are lots of other hidden costs involved with "finishing" your Bolognese, that is, making him a champion. Things like equipment, travel, training and conditioning all cost money.

Many owners, on the other hand, enter their "average" Bolognese in dog shows for the fun and enjoyment of it. If both dog and owner enjoy it, dog showing makes an absorbing hobby with many rewards for canine and human participants alike. If you're having fun, meeting other people who share your interests and enjoying the overall experience, you likely will

second oldest and second largest all-breed dog registry, attracting around 250,000 registrations each year. Chauncey Z. Bennett founded the UKC in 1898 with an aim to support the "total dog," meaning a dog that possesses quality in physical conformation and performance alike. With that in mind, the UKC sponsors competitive events that emphasize

Although the dogs are lined up side by side, the judge is comparing each entry to the breed standard, not to the other dogs in the ring.

catch the "bug." Once the dog-show bug bites, its effects can last a lifetime; it's much better than a deer tick! Soon you will be envisioning yourself in the center ring at a prestigious rare-breed show!

RARE-BREED SHOWING

MEET THE UNITED KENNEL CLUB
Rare breeds in the United States have many opportunities to compete in conformation showing and other events. A glance at the United Kennel Club (UKC) website (www.ukcdogs.com) tells us that the UKC is America's

CLASSES AT UNITED KENNEL CLUB DOG SHOWS

The Regular classes, for all dogs who are not Champions or Grand Champions, are divided by sex (and variety) with four winners selected by the judge. Champions and Grand Champions are judged separately, with one winner in each class. The Regular classes are broken down into the following:

Puppy Class: Male and female puppies, from six months to under one year of age.

Junior Class: Male and female dogs, from one year to under two years of age.

Senior Class: Male and female dogs, from two years of age to under three years of age.

Adult Class: Male and female dogs, three years of age and older.

Breeder/Handler Class: Male and female dogs, six months of age and older, handled by the breeder of record or a member of the breeder's immediate family.

this "total dog" aspect. Along with traditional conformation shows, the UKC's performance events encompass just about every skill that one could imagine in a dog. These performance events include obedience, agility, coonhound trials, water races, hunting tests designed for specific types of dog (retrievers, Beagles, curs and feists, etc.) and much more. The website goes on to say, "Essentially, the UKC world of dogs is a working world. That's the way founder Chauncey Bennett designed it, and that's the way it remains today." Although the Bolognese is a companion and not a working breed, he is suited for obedience and agility events along with conformation competition.

What many think of as traditional "dog shows" are more formally known as conformation shows. These are competitive events in which dogs are evaluated based on their conformation to their breed's standard, which is the official written description of the ideal representative of that breed. The standards recognized by the UKC are either adopted from those of Europe's canine registry, the Fédération Cynologique Internationale (FCI), or submitted by the American breed club and then revised and adopted by the UKC. At many shows, handlers will receive verbal "critiques" of their dogs;

these critiques may always be requested if not given automatically. This critique details a dog's comparison to the breed standard, and the judge also will explain why he placed each dog as he did.

UKC dog shows may be held for one breed only, several breeds or all breeds. UKC shows are arranged differently than the conformation shows of other organizations. Entries are restricted by age, and you cannot show your dog in a class other than his correct age class. When you compete for championship points, you may enter Puppy, Junior, Senior or Adult age

A dog's gait reveals a lot about his proper body conformation. A Bolognese should have an energetic gait with his head held high.

classes. You may also enter the Breeder/Handler Class, where dogs six months of age or older compete, but the dog must be handled by his breeder or a member of the breeder's immediate family. The winners of each class compete for Best Male or Best Female. These two dogs then compete for Best of Winners; the dog who is given this award will go on to compete for Best of Breed. Best of Breed competition includes the Best of Winners and dogs that have earned Champion and Grand Champion titles. Earning Best Male or Best Female, as long as there is competition, is considered a "major."

Once a dog has earned 3 "majors" and accumulated 100 points, he is considered a UKC Champion. What this means is that the dog is now ready to compete for the title of Grand Champion, which is equivalent to an AKC championship. To earn the Grand Champion title, a dog must compete with a minimum of two other dogs who are also Champions. The dog must win this class, called the Champion of Champions class, five times under three different judges. In rare breeds, it is difficult to assemble a class of Champions, so the UKC Grand Champion title is truly a prestigious one. Once a dog has earned the Grand Champion title, he can continue to compete for Top Ten, but there are no further

titles to earn. "Top Ten" refers to the ten dogs in each breed that have won the most points in a given year. These dogs compete in a Top Ten invitational competition annually.

Depending on the show-giving club, Group competition may or may not be offered. The Bolognese is classified in the UKC's Group 8, Companion Dogs. A Group must have a minimum of five breeds entered in order for Group competition to take place. If Group competition is offered, Best in Show consists of the Group winners. If there is no Group competition, then all Best of Breed dogs go into the ring at the same time to compete for Best in Show. This can be a large number of dogs and thus can be very interesting, to say the least!

Aside from the variations already presented, UKC shows differ from other dog shows in one very significant way: no professional handlers are allowed to show dogs, except for those dogs they own themselves. UKC shows create an atmosphere that is owner-friendly, relaxed and genuine fun. Bait in the ring is allowed at the discretion of the judge, but throwing the bait, dropping it on the floor or other "handler tricks" will get an owner excused from the ring in a big hurry.

In addition to conformation dog shows, the UKC offers many

more venues for dogs and their owners, in keeping with their mission to promote the "total dog." Obedience and agility competition are suitable for the Bolognese, and the UKC offers other events, such as hunting and weight pulling, geared toward other types of dogs.

Mrs. Helen Whitehouse Walker, a Standard Poodle fancier, can be credited with introducing obedience trials to the United States. In the 1930s she designed a series of exercises based on those of the Associated Sheep, Police, Army Dog Society of Great Britain. These exercises were intended to evaluate the working relationship between dog and owner. Since those early days of the sport in the US, obedience trials have grown more and more popular, and now more than 2,000 trials each year attract over 100,000 dogs and their owners.

UKC obedience events test the training of dogs as they perform a series of prescribed exercises at the commands of their handlers. There are several levels of competition, ranging from basic commands such as "sit," "come" and "heel," to advanced exercises like scent discrimination and directed retrieves over jumps, based on the dog's level of accomplishment. The classes are further delineated by the experience of the handler.

UKC obedience differs from AKC obedience in many respects. Even at the most basic levels, the dogs are expected to "honor"

JUNIOR SHOWMANSHIP

For budding dog handlers, junior showmanship competitions are excellent training for the up-and-coming generation of exhibitors. Owning and caring for a dog are wonderful methods of teaching children responsibility, and junior showmanship builds upon that foundation. Junior handlers learn by grooming, handling and training their dogs, and the quality of a junior's presentation of the dog (and himself) is evaluated by a licensed judge.

The United Kennel Club's Junior Program welcomes young handlers to experience many aspects of the dog sport through participation in performance events like agility, obedience and weight pulling, as well as traditional conformation showing, embracing the UKC's concept of the "total dog." Juniors from ages 2 to 18 are recognized for their achievements in these areas of the dog sport. Good sportmanship is emphasized in all areas of the Junior Program, as well as adherence to the rules and regulations, responsible ownership and humane training.

To gain experience and knowledge, junior handlers are encouraged to join dog clubs and seek advice from those more experienced. For more information, rules of the program and an application for membership, visit www.ukcdogs.com/TotalJuniorProgram.htm.

other dogs who are working. In other words, the "honoring" dog must be placed in a down/stay while his owner leaves the ring and moves out of sight. The dog must remain in the down/stay position while the working dog goes through the heeling exercises.

Agility events are fast-paced exercises in which the handler directs his dog through a course involving tunnels, sway bridges, jumps and other obstacles in a race against the clock. The dogs are scored according to the manner in which they negotiate the obstacles and the time elapsed to complete the course. UKC agility is very similar to AKC agility; clubs often will offer both AKC and UKC agility events (not on the same day). There are other competitive events offered by the UKC, including hunting and weight pulling, in which the Bolognese does not compete.

The first organization to promote agility trials in the US was the United States Dog Agility Association, Inc. (USDAA). Established in 1986, the USDAA sparked the formation of many member clubs around the country. To participate in USDAA trials, dogs must be at least 18 months of

Although competitive, dog shows are also wonderful social events where people can meet others who share their love of the breed and the sport.

EUROPEAN BREEDING CLUBS

The history of dog-breeding clubs is marked by a multitude of changes. The individual clubs have always been members of higher organizations. This is also true for the Verband Deutscher Kleinhundzüchter e.V. (VK), founded in 1948, which is a member of the Verband für das Deutsche Hundewesen e.V. (VDH) with its head office in Dortmund. The VDH, in turn, is a full member of the world dog-breeding organization, the Fédération Cynologique Internationale (FCI) with its head office in Thuin, Belgium. The FCI comprises 80 countries, which are either full members, associate members or contract partners. These members each issue their own pedigrees and train their own judges. The FCI ensures that all of their members mutually recognize these pedigrees and judges. The acceptance of new dog-breeding clubs is governed by strict rules. The pedigree registries of the VK are all imprinted with the authentication VDH-FCI. This organization takes care of Bolognese breeders and another 12 breeding clubs of small dog breeds. Besides the VDH there are a number of other dog-breeding clubs which all conform to the generally accepted breed standards issued by the FCI, including the UCI, EHU, AKC and more.

Besides the Bolognese the VK-VDH represents another 12 breeds of small dogs, e.g., Bichon Frise, Cavalier King Charles Spaniel, Chihuahua, Havanese, Löwchen, Maltese, Pug, Papillon, Phalene, Schipperke, Shih Tzu and Brussels Griffon.

age. The USDAA offers its own titles to winning dogs: Agility Dog (AD), Advanced Agility Dog (AAD) and Master Agility Dog (MAD).

Agility trials are a great way to keep your dog active, and they will keep you running, too! You should join a local agility club to learn more about the sport. These clubs offer sessions in which you can introduce your dog to the various obstacles as well as training classes to prepare him for competition. In no time, your dog will be climbing A-frames, crossing the dog walk and flying over hurdles, all with you right beside him. Your heart will leap every time your dog jumps through the hoop—and you'll be having just as much (if not more) fun!

OTHER RARE-BREED ORGANIZATIONS
In addition to the United Kennel Club, there are several other organizations that offer registration and competitive events for rare breeds. The availability of these depends on geography. The IABCA (International All-Breed Canine Association of America) holds conformation shows under FCI rules. This club offers both American and international

DRESS THE PART

It's a dog show, so don't forget your costume. Even though the show is about the dog, you also must play your role well. You have been cast as the "dog handler" and you must smartly dress the part. Solid colors make a nice complement to the dog's coat, but choose colors that contrast. You don't want to be wearing a solid color that blends mostly or entirely with the major or only color of your dog. Whether the show is indoors or out, you still must dress properly. You want the judge to perceive you as being professional, so polish, polish, polish! And don't forget to wear sensible shoes; remember, you have to gait around the ring with your dog.

judges at all of their shows. Most of their events are held in the western US but now also are offered in both the Midwest and Florida.

As with UKC shows, IABCA shows divide dogs by age. Dogs are considered "puppies" up to 18 months of age for large breeds and up to 15 months of age for smaller breeds. You cannot enter your dog in any class except the appropriate class for his age. After puppyhood, you can enter your dog in the adult class. Once your dog has earned his championship, he goes on to compete for various ranks of champion, of which there are too many to enumerate. There

are fun classes as well, one of which is "Best Rare Breed in Show." This class is only offered on the Sunday of a show weekend, and only those dogs earning the highest award possible in their classes may enter (Best Puppy, Best of Breed).

In order for a dog to earn a championship, he must receive three V-1 ratings. Each dog is given a written critique during the class. The judge will ask the handler to stand near the judges' table and will either make notes or dictate to the ring steward as he compares your dog to the standard. A handler can listen while the judge does this, and often the judge will ask questions, especially of handlers showing rare-breed dogs. It is a very interesting and educational procedure, to say the least. Rare breeds can earn a championship without competing against other dogs, because the dog is always competing against the breed standard. There are times when no dog in a breed receives a V-1 if none is of sufficient quality to warrant such a rating.

Another organization, the American Rare Breed Association (ARBA), holds shows across the country, although not in great numbers. In ARBA competition, as in IABCA competition, a dog can win points and earn his championship by showing against the standard, not necessarily against other dogs. ARBA's major show, the Cherry Blossom show, which is held annually in Washington, DC each spring, draws a handsome entry.

A show-giving group called Rarities, Inc. has also arrived on the scene in the United States and Canada. This group is dedicated to the support of ancient and rare breeds. To obtain a championship, a dog requires 15 points. Of these 15 points, the dog must have attained 2 "majors" of at least 3 points under 2 different judges; further, the total of 15 points must have been obtained under 3 different judges. Shows with double points awarded count toward both the American and Canadian championship. To earn the international championship, the dog must win both the American and Canadian championships. The Grand Champion

WHAT IS THE FCI?

The FCI *does not* issue pedigrees. The FCI members and contract partners are responsible for issuing pedigrees and training judges in their own countries. The FCI does maintain a list of judges and makes sure that they are recognized throughout the FCI member countries.

The FCI also *does not* act as a breeder referral; breeder information is available from FCI-recognized national canine societies in each of the FCI's member countries.

title is earned by defeating 15 other Rarities or FCI champions. Grand Champions (not pending Grand Champions) may compete for the title Supreme Grand Champion, which is earned by defeating 15 other Rarities Grand Champions. In Rarities shows, as in UKC shows, a dog must defeat other dogs in order to earn a championship. One of the unique things about Rarities, Inc. is that all Working Group breeds must also pass a temperament test, although this of course does not apply to the Bolognese.

FÉDÉRATION CYNOLOGIQUE INTERNATIONALE

The Fédération Cynologique Internationale (FCI) aims to encourage and promote breeding and use of pure-bred dogs that properly represent their breed standards and are capable of working in their bred-for capacities, as well as to protect the breeding and keeping of dogs around the world and to support the open exchange of dogs and information between member countries. Founded on May 22, 1911, the FCI today operates around the world, in 79 member countries divided into 5 regional groups, which include Europe; the Americas and the Caribbean; Asia; Africa; and Oceania and Australia. When the organization was established it included only five countries: Germany, Austria,

France, the Netherlands and Belgium. The Société Royale Saint-Hubert of Belgium deserves credit for recreating the organization in 1921 after it disappeared during World War I.

Recognizing over 330 breeds, nearly twice the number of any other registry, the FCI considers each breed as the "property" of its native country and recognizes the breed standard of the country of origin. All 79 member countries conduct both International Shows and Working/Hunting Trials. National shows are held, though these are governed by the rules of the member country and not the FCI.

FCI conformation shows are sometimes called "beauty shows" and differ in many respects to the shows of other kennel clubs. For example, each dog is critiqued by the judge in writing, and these "judge's reports" are available to the exhibitor. The judge must detail his evaluation and designate a grade to the dog, based entirely on conformation to the standard. This process is far more time-consuming than that of other kennel clubs and also demands that the judge be able to "document" his decision for placing the dog first or last. The judges assign the following qualifications to dogs: Excellent (close to ideal, excellent condition, good balance and superior presentation), Very Good (typical of breed and well balanced, with a few minor faults), Good (most breed characteristics with faults), Sufficient or Satisfactory (correspond to breed but not typical), Disqualified (atypical with serious faults) and Cannot Be Judged (uncontrolled in ring).

The FCI's most prestigious shows are the all-breed shows, such as the World Dog Show, followed by the sections shows, like the European Dog Show and the International Championship Shows. National shows can be all-

TEN GROUPS
The FCI is divided into ten groups that classify the breeds by traditional functions. The official breed list indicates whether or not the breed requires a Working Trial in order to earn the CACIB title.
Group 1: Sheepdogs and Cattledogs (except Swiss Cattledogs)
Group 2: Pinschers and Schnauzers, Molossians, Swiss Mountain Dogs and Swiss Cattledogs
Group 3: Terriers
Group 4: Dachshunds
Group 5: Spitz- and primitive-type dogs
Group 6: Scenthounds and related breeds
Group 7: Pointing dogs
Group 8: Retrievers, Flushing dogs and Water dogs
Group 9: Companion and Toy dogs
Group 10: Sighthounds

breed shows, Group Championship Shows, Breed or Specialty Shows, Open Shows, Club Shows and Young Dog Shows. At all of these shows, dog can earn World or European Championship titles or the CACIB certificate. The *Certificat d'Aptitude au Championnat International de Beauté* (CACIB) is the international certificate won by dogs; the national certificate is known as the *Certificat d'Aptitude au Championnat National de Beauté* (CAC). The judge awards the CACIB certificate to a superior dog in the Open, Working or Champion Class. A dog that has won four CACIBs (without Working or Hunting Trial) is designated an International Beauty Champion, provided that the certificates were won in three different countries, one of which must be the country of residence or origin. The title of National Beauty Champion is awarded to a dog who has earned two, three or four CACs, depending on the country. The titles International Champion and National Champion are reserved only for those breeds that must undergo Working or Hunting Trials.

The following classes are offered at FCI shows: Puppy Class (6–9 months of age), Junior Class (9–18 months of age), Intermediate Class (15–24 months of age), Open Class, Working Class, Champion Class (these latter 3, all 15 months of age and over) and Veterans Class (8 years of age and over).

For more information about the FCI, show schedules and rules and regulations, you can visit the website at www.fci.be. The FCI also publishes the *Trimestrial Magazine* in four languages (French, English, German and Spanish). Contact Stratego, Muhlenweg 4, 7221 Marz, Austria for information about the magazine.

SO MUCH TO DO!

The bottom line is this: There is so much to do with your dog that it can be hard to decide which event to try! Just as we have to choose what to do with our weekends, so do the dogs. Whatever you choose to do with your dog, it will take training, dedication and a willingness to work with your dog to achieve a common goal, a partnership between you and your dog. There is nothing more pleasing than to watch a handler and dog performing at a high level, whether it is the show ring or the field. There is something for everyone and every dog in the world of dog "showing." Dog showing should really be called "competing with your dog." You are not restricted to the traditional "dog show" and may find that your "show dog" excels in other areas as well or instead.

INDEX

*Page numbers in **boldface** indicate illustrations.*

Activity 29, 33, 110
—level 76
Adult dog
—adoption 93
—health 115
—training 92-93
Adult Class 146-147
Airplane travel 89, 90
Aggression 66, 94, 108, 122
Agility events 34, 110, 150-151
Aging 117
Alpha role 101
Amanda Di Chiesanova **26**
American Heartworm Society 137
American Kennel Club 21, 24, 40
—address 144
—Foundation Stock Service 25
American Rare Breed Association 25, 44, 152
—shows 153
Anal gland 86
Ancylostoma caninum **133, 136**
Antifreeze 57, 118
Appearance 32
Appetite loss 72, 118
Ascarid **132, 133**
Ascaris lumbricoides **132**
Aspen Villa Bolognese 24
Attention 101-102, 107
Bait 148
Band Wag-on, The 25
Barking 28
Bathing 81-84
Beard 84
Beauty shows 154
Bedding 52, 59, 97
Belair, Carrie 25
Bennett, Chauncey Z. 146-147
Berdot Havanese kennels 22
Berlin Wall 16
Best Female 148
Best in Show 148
Best Male 148
Best of Breed 148
Best of Winners 148
Best Rare Breed in Show 152
Bichon bolognais 10
Bichon Bolognese Association of America 25
Bichon Frise **16**, 17, 19
Bichon Ténérife 20
Bichonner 10
Blanquitto de la Habana 20
Bloat 118
Boarding 91
Body language 94, 98
Body temperature 123
Bologna 10
Bolognese Club of America 24, 44

Bolognese Club of Canada 25
Bolonka Franzuska 14, **15**, 16
Bolonka Zwetna **14, 15**
Bolshevik Revolution 13
Bones 53, 71
Bordetella bronchiseptica 121
Borreliosis 121
Bowls 51
Breed club 45, 147
Breed purpose 28
Breed standard 36, 40, 46, 147
Breeder 45, 68
—selection 44-46, 49, 113
Breeder/Handler Class 146-147
British Bolognese Club 44
Brize Cesky Dukat 26
Brushing 76
Brushing teeth 86
Canadian Kennel Club 144
Cancer 122, 138
Canine Eye Registration Foundation 25
Canine Good Citizen® 33, 145
Car travel 89, 108
Cat introductions 67
Catharine the Great 10
Certificat d'Aptitude au Championnat International de Beauté 155
Certificat d'Aptitude au Championnat National de Beauté 155
Champion 146, 148
Champion of Champions 148
Character 31
Chemicals 75
Chew toys 52-53, 63, 64, 96, 98
Chewing 52, 63, 108
Cheyletiella mite **129**
Chiggers 131
Children 35, 59-60, 63, 94, 108
Classes at shows 146-147
—FCI 155
Clipping 32, 80
Clochards 19
Coat 32, 33
Cognitive dysfunction 117, 139
Collar 54, 88, 102, 108
Color 19, 21, 32
Combing 76, 78
Come 103, 107-108
Commands 66, 78, 103
—practicing 104, 106
Commitment of ownership 49-50
Competitive events
—UKC 146
Conformation showing 145, 154
—classes at 147
Consistency 61, 66

Core vaccines 121
Coronavirus 121
Correction 101
Cost 49
Coton de Réunion 20
Coton de Tuléar **19**, 20
Crate 51, 59, 65, 96
—pad 52
—training 52, 94, 100
Critique 147, 152, 154
Crying 59, 65, 97
Ctenocephalides canis **124**
Dangers in the home 55, 57
Davis, Peggy 36
De la Bathiére kennel 19
Dé Medici, Cosimo 10
De Pompadour, Madame la Marquise 10
DEET 131
Demodex mite **131**
Demodicosis 130-131
Dental care 115, 117
Dental health 118
Dental problems 72
Dentition 86
Desfarges, Carmen 19
Diet 68-74
Dipylidium caninum 134, **136**
Dirofilaria immitis 135, **136, 137**
Discipline 62, 100, 101
Distemper 121
Dog club 45
Dog flea 124
Dogfight 108
Dominance 104
Down 98, 104
Down/stay 106
Dry baths 84
Ear mite 129-131
Ears 83
Echinococcus multilocularis 135
Eggs 71
Elizabeth of Manchukuo, Empress **11**
Emergency care 118
England, Marsha 27
Épagneuls 20-21
Estrus 122
Europe 23
European Dog Show 154
Excessive thirst 73
Exercise 75, 76
—pen 95
Expenses of ownership 49
External parasites 124-131
Eyes 83
Fabiola Von Albany **25**
Family meeting the puppy 58
Fatima's Bolognese 25, 27
Fear period 61

Federal Republic of Germany 15
Fédération Cynologique Internationale 14, 15, 25, 36, 44, 144, 147, 153-154
Feeding 66, 68-74
—schedule 70
Fenced yard 57, 108
Fertilizers 75
First aid 118
Fleas **124**, 125, **126**
Food 69, 71, 96
—bowls 51
—forms of 73
—guarding 66
—lack of interest in 72, 118
—quantity 74
—raw 71
—rewards 92, 109
Gaiting 142
Garayalde, Barbara 27
Genetic testing 113
German Democratic Republic 15
Gonzagas 10
Goodale, Dorothy 22-26
Gozzoli 10
Grand Champion 146, 148, 153
Grass 75
Grooming 31, 33, 76-87
Group competition 148
Handler 144, 148, 152
Havanese 19, **20**-22, 24
Health 57
—adult 115
—insurance for pets 119
—journal 58
—problems 45
—puppy 113
—senior dog 117
Heart disease 117
Heartworm 115, 135, **136, 137**
Heat cycle 46-48, 122
Heel 108-109
Height 30, 31
Hepatitis 121
Hesseltvan Dinter, Johan and Diane 25-26
Heterodoxus spiniger **130**
Hillebrecht, Dr. 22
Homemade toys 54
Hookworm **133, 136**
House-training 51-52, 67, 94, 99-100
—puppy needs 94
—schedule 100
Hunting Trial 154
Identification 87, 88
Infectious diseases 121
Insurance 119
Internal parasites 132-137

International All-Breed Canine Association of America 44, 151
—shows 152
International Beauty Champion 155
International certificate 155
International Champion 155
International Championship Show 154
International Show 154
Ixodes dammini **127-128**
Ja-Birs kennels 23
Judge's report 154
Jumping up 98
Junior Class 146-147
Junior showmanship 149
K'Bella Bolognese 25
Kennel Club, The 44, 144
Kennel de la Buthière 19
Kidney problems 117
Kindergarten classes 101
Leash 55, 102
—pulling on 109
Leave it 108
Leptospira 121
Lifespan 115
Litter size 48-49
Liver 71
Lost dog 88
Louis XIV 10
Louis XV 10
Louse **130**
Löwchen 19, 21-**22**
Lyme disease 121
Majors 148, 153
Maltese **17**, 19
Mammary cancer 122
Markings 19
Mats 76, 77
Meat 71
Microchipping 88
Milk 71, 75
Mites **129**, 130, **131**
Mosquitoes 131, 135, 137
Motion sickness 89
Mounting 122
Nail clipping 84
Name 102, 108
National Beauty Champion 155
National certificate 155
National Champion 155
Neutering 115, 122
Nipping 63
Non-core vaccines 121
Nuntius 10
Nutrition 73
Obedience 105
—classes 101, 109
—events 149
—trials 110
Off 98
Ogno, Sna. Maristella 13
Okay 105, 107, 109
Old-dog syndrome 139

Original purpose 10
Origins 9
Other pets 66, 67, 94
Otodectes cynotis **129**
Outdoor safety 57
Ovariohysterectomy 122
Ownership 29, 49-50
—expenses of 49
Pack animals 61
Paper-training 94, 98
Parainfluenza 121
Parasites 57
—external 124-131
—internal 132-137
Parvovirus 121
Patience 93
Pedigree 46, 60
Peronda, Carla 23
Personality 28
Physical development 69
Plants 55, 118
Playtime 107
Poisons 55, 57, 75, 118
Positive reinforcement 59, 101, 103
Possessive behavior 66
Practicing commands 104, 106
Praise 93, 101, 109
Prelude to Joy Bolognese 27
Prelude to Joy Gilligan **28**
Preventive care 113, 115, 117
Proglottid **135**
Prostate problems 122
Punishment 65, 100-101
Puppy
—common problems 62
—diet 68
—establishing leadership 92
—first night in new home 59
—health 113
—kindergarten class 102
—meeting the family 58
—parasites 57
—personality 49, 115
—proofing 55
—selection 44-46, 49, 113
—show quality 46, 144-145
—socialization 60
—supplies for 50
—teething 64
—training 62, 92
Puppy class 146-147
Rabies 121
Rare breeds 146
Rare-Breed organizations 146, 151
Rarities, Inc. 153
Rawhide 53
Regular classes 146
Renaissance Bolognese 27
Rewards 93, 100, 101, 109
—food 101
Rhabditis **136**
Roaming 122

Rope toys 54
Roundworm 57, **132**, 133, **136**
Roxanne 27
Russia 13-17
Safety 51, 55, 75, 95, 98, 107-108
—commands 108
—in the car 108
—outdoors 57
Sarcoptes scabiei **129**
Scabies 129
Scent attraction 99
Scheetz, Melissa 24
Selection 44-46
Senior Class 146
Senior dog 115
—health 117
Sex differences 46-48
Shampoo 81
Shopping for puppy needs 50
Show quality 46, 144, 145
Shows 140-145
Sit 103
Sit/stay 105
Size 30, 36
Slicker brush 76
Socialization 46, 60, 62, 101-102, 115
Société Royale Saint-Hubert 153
Soft toys 53
Sopra Villa kennel 27
Spaying 115, 122
Spice of Life Bolognese 25
Spice of Life Estella Expectation **27**
Spot bath 84
Stay 105
Stray dog 88
Suitable owners 29
Sularo, Sre. 36
Supervision 62, 64, 98
Supreme Grand Champion 153
Surgery 122
Table scraps 71
Taenia pisiformis **135**
Tapeworm 134, **135**, **136**
Tartar 86
Tattooing 88
Teeth 115, 117-118
Teething 63, 64
Temperament evaluation 115
Temperature, taking your dog's 123
Testicular cancer 122
Therapy dog 110
Therese, Maria 10
Thirst 73
Tick-borne diseases 127
Ticks **127-128**
Timing 99, 107
Todman, Sharon 25, 27
Toxascaris leonine 132
Toxins 55, 57, 71, 75, 118
Toxocara canis **132**

Toys 52, 53, 63-64, 96, 98
Training 31, 102
—basic principles 92
—commands 103
—consistency in 61, 66
—crate 52, 94, 100
—early 62
—getting started 102
—importance of timing 99, 107
—tips 62
Traveling 51, 89, 90, 97, 108
Treats 59, 93, 101
—weaning off in training 109
Trichuris sp. **134**
Tricks 110
Trimestrial Magazine 155
Type 144-145
Union of Soviet Socialist Republics 14-15
United Kennel Club 25, 44, 146, 147
—address 144
—Junior Program 149
—titles 148
United States 22
United States Dog Agility Association, Inc. 150
—titles 151
Urine marking 122
V-1 ratings 152
Vaccinations 58, 61, 115, 121
Van Het Vogelpark kennels 23
Vansteenkiste-Delen, Madame Gerde 23
Vansteenkiste kennels 23
Verbandes für das Deutsche Hundewesen 17
Veronesi, Alberto 23
Veterinarian 45, 53-54, 57, 108, 115, 117-119
Veterinary insurance 119
Visiting the litter 49
Vitamin A toxicity 71
Vitamin supplementation 69
Wait 108
Walker, Mrs. Helen Whitehouse 149
Warming, Jan and Birte 23
Watchdog 28
Water 67, 74, 75, 96
—bowls 51
—increased intake 73
Weight 25, 30, 31
West Nile virus 131
Whining 59, 65, 97
Whipworm **134**
Working Trial 154
World Dog Show 154
World War I 154
World War II 13, 23
Worm control 134
Worming treatment 57
Yard 57
Zwinger und Feld 22

My Bolognese

PUT YOUR PUPPY'S FIRST PICTURE HERE

Dog's Name Daisy Mae Roberts

Date _____ Photographer _____